MW00445930

The Poverty Paradox

The Poverty Paradox

Understanding Economic Hardship

Amid American Prosperity

MARK ROBERT RANK

OXFORD
UNIVERSITY PRESS

OXFORD
UNIVERSITY PRESS

Oxford University Press is a department of the University of Oxford. It furthers
the University's objective of excellence in research, scholarship, and education
by publishing worldwide. Oxford is a registered trade mark of Oxford University
Press in the UK and certain other countries.

Published in the United States of America by Oxford University Press
198 Madison Avenue, New York, NY 10016, United States of America.

© Oxford University Press 2023

All rights reserved. No part of this publication may be reproduced, stored in
a retrieval system, or transmitted, in any form or by any means, without the
prior permission in writing of Oxford University Press, or as expressly permitted
by law, by license, or under terms agreed with the appropriate reproduction
rights organization. Inquiries concerning reproduction outside the scope of the
above should be sent to the Rights Department, Oxford University Press, at the
address above.

You must not circulate this work in any other form
and you must impose this same condition on any acquirer.

Library of Congress Cataloging-in-Publication Data
Names: Rank, Mark Robert, author.
Title: The poverty paradox : understanding economic hardship amid American prosperity /
Mark Robert Rank
Description: New York, NY : Oxford University Press, [2023] |
Includes bibliographical references and index. |
Identifiers: LCCN 2022044695 (print) | LCCN 2022044696 (ebook) |
ISBN 9780190212636 (hardback) | ISBN 9780190212650 (epub) |
ISBN 9780197677513 (oso)
Subjects: LCSH: Poverty—United States. | United States—Social policy.
Classification: LCC HC110.P6 M317 2023 (print) | LCC HC110.P6 (ebook) |
DDC 362.5/560973—dc23/eng/20221026
LC record available at https://lccn.loc.gov/2022044695
LC ebook record available at https://lccn.loc.gov/2022044696

DOI: 10.1093/oso/9780190212636.001.0001

Printed by Sheridan Books, Inc., United States of America

CONTENTS

PART I

Overview

1

Introduction

This book has been quite some time in the making. Across a number of years, I have researched, taught, and written about poverty. In my opinion, there are few topics of greater importance. It is a dominant and disturbing feature of the American landscape. Yet, despite the hundreds of books, articles, reports, and programs addressing the issue, the United States continues to have the highest rates of poverty among the wealthy countries.

The question is, why? Why should a nation with the resources that America possesses be plagued by the amount of poverty it has? The paradox of poverty amid prosperity has puzzled social commentators for decades.

Central to this puzzle has been the question of causality. It is fundamental to understanding this troublesome subject. What causes poverty, and why does it persist? Much of the debate in America has been rooted in the question of causation. How we choose to address poverty is highly dependent on what we view the reasons to be.

In the United States, the causes of poverty have typically been thought to lie within the control and behavior of individuals. Consequently, those who are poor are perceived as less motivated, as possessing lower levels of ability, having made bad decisions in their life, and so forth. On the other hand, those who do well economically are viewed as hard working, having considerable ability and talent, and exerting good decision-making throughout their lives. There is a sense of deservedness embedded in this perspective: Those who do well deserve it, and those who do not likewise deserve their fate.

I argue in the pages ahead that such a viewpoint is inadequate for explaining poverty. Rather, what I have called a structural vulnerability explanation of poverty is developed. Simply put, the argument is that poverty ultimately results from failures at the economic and political levels. There are not nearly enough opportunities and resources to support the entire population. This is the fallout of both free market capitalism and political decision-making. The label itself combines two key elements of the theory. First, poverty is ultimately structural in nature. Second, a large number of individuals and families are economically vulnerable as a result.

I first outlined the structural vulnerability perspective in my 1994 book, *Living on the Edge: The Realities of Welfare in America*, where I sought to understand the realities of surviving on the social safety net as opposed to the stereotypes and myths surrounding the issue.[1] Through dozens of interviews with welfare recipients, it became clear that these were individuals who had worked hard their entire life and wanted the best for their families. The explanation of laziness or lack of motivation did not seem to apply to the vast majority of women and men I talked to.

Ten years later, I examined the topic of poverty in greater detail in the book, *One Nation, Underprivileged: Why American Poverty Affects Us All*.[2] The emphasis here was on developing a new paradigm for understanding poverty, including the structural vulnerability framework.

A third book, *Chasing the American Dream: Understanding What Shapes Our Fortunes*, explored the meaning and pursuit of the American Dream.[3] Once again, aspects of the structural vulnerability perspective were used to shed light on the dynamics of economic fortune and misfortune.

Most recently, in the book *Poorly Understood: What America Gets Wrong About Poverty*, my coauthors and I discussed the various myths and misconceptions surrounding American poverty.[4] We argued that poverty is an issue that has been widely misunderstood by the America public.

In *The Poverty Paradox* I turn to the manner in which I believe we should understand such poverty, rather than continuing with our stereotypes. The book is divided into three sections. Part I is designed to provide a background into the dynamics of poverty, as well as how Americans have traditionally viewed poverty. Chapter 2 reviews some of the ways in which we can conceptualize and measure poverty, along with data on the overall likelihood of poverty. Chapter 3 explores what we might call the traditional American perspective, which is grounded in an idealized image of a society with abundant opportunities, where hard work is rewarded by economic prosperity. Poverty is therefore seen as largely the fault of the individual: Anyone willing to work hard should be able to avoid poverty. Several prominent social science theories are also discussed.

In Part II, the structural vulnerability framework is described in detail. This perspective stands in sharp contrast with the traditional ways we have understood poverty. Each chapter covers a different component of the model. In Chapter 4, it is argued that essential to an initial understanding of poverty is the concept of economic vulnerability and an awareness of the importance of the lack of human capital in accentuating such vulnerability. Individuals more likely to experience poverty tend to have characteristics that put them at a disadvantage in terms of their earning ability within the labor market. These include factors such as fewer marketable skills and less education.

Given that education and skills bear on poverty (by causing varying degrees of vulnerability), why are individuals lacking these in the first place? Chapter 5 posits that a major reason is the role of cumulative inequality. This is the second component of the structural vulnerability framework. The chapter details how social class differences beginning at birth often result in the process of cumulative inequality, leading individuals to having greater or lesser amounts of human capital and therefore having a greater or lesser likelihood of experiencing poverty.

A third component of the structural vulnerability perspective is the realization that there are two levels to understanding impoverishment. Chapter 6 takes up this issue. On the one hand, we can identify who is more likely to experience poverty by understanding the impact that human capital has on individual economic vulnerability. On the other hand, we can ascertain why poverty occurs in the first place by looking at the wider structural failings that occur within the United States. These include failings at both the economic and political levels. Our economy simply does not provide enough decent-paying jobs for all in society, and our social policies fail to protect individuals from falling into poverty. Chapter 6 concludes by pulling together these three components of the structural vulnerability perspective and discusses the framework as a whole.

In Part III, the final section of the book, I apply the structural vulnerability perspective to the wider social and policy context. Chapter 7 ties the structural vulnerability perspective to several core values that the policy ideas in Chapter 8 are built on. The importance of reinforcing a set of key principles is accomplished by addressing the dynamics of poverty outlined in the structural vulnerability model.

In Chapter 8, various policy ideas are laid out that can effectively reduce the extent of poverty and economic inequality. They follow logically from the structural vulnerability understanding of poverty. These policies include ensuring that jobs pay a livable wage, providing a robust safety net, increasing access to key public resources, building assets, and organizing. The book concludes in Chapter 9 with some thoughts about moving a structural vulnerability understanding of poverty forward into the future.

Understanding why poverty exists is fundamental to solving this blight on the landscape. As I have argued in earlier work, poverty affects and undermines us all. Yet too often we fail to understand the true nature of poverty. This misunderstanding helps to explain the paradox of poverty within a land of plenty. As a nation we can and must do better.

Defining, Measuring, and Counting

A logical starting point to begin our exploration of poverty is to examine various ways of defining and measuring impoverishment. Moreover, how many people are considered poor in the United States and for how long do they remain there? Finally, what background characteristics define those in poverty? Reviewing the scope and dynamics of a problem is always an excellent place to set about an initial understanding of an issue.

DEFINING POVERTY

Over the centuries, poverty has been conceptualized and defined in a number of different ways. In ancient societies, the poor were often thought of as those who fell into particularly unfortunate categories, such as beggars, the sick, or the widowed. In medieval times, those in poverty would have been considered the peasant class, which encompassed most of society.

More recently, Adam Smith in his 1776 landmark treatise, *The Wealth of Nations*, defined poverty as a lack of those necessities that "the custom of the country renders it indecent for creditable people, even of the lowest order, to be without."[1] This type of definition is what is known as an absolute approach to defining poverty. A minimum threshold for adequate living conditions is determined, and individuals falling below that threshold are considered poor.

On its surface, many of us might agree with Smith's description. However, our consensus would probably begin to break down over what exactly such necessities should encompass. Certainly most of us would include items such as food, clothing, and shelter, but what kind of food, clothing, and shelter? Furthermore, what additional items might we include—a smart phone, health insurance, internet access, a car, and so on?

If we turn to the dictionary for contemporary guidance in defining poverty, Webster defined poverty in three ways: "1. the state or condition of having little or no money, goods, or means of support; 2. deficiency of necessary or desirable ingredients, qualities, etc.; 3. scantiness; insufficiency." Here again we have the notion that poverty consists of a shortage of basic goods and resources, and that the lack of money is the cause of this shortage. Similarly, the World Bank defined poverty as: "A person is considered poor if his or her income level fall below some minimum level necessary to meet basic needs."[2]

Yet another way of thinking about how we might define poverty is to conceptualize what such a shortage means in the daily lives of individuals. It is within this context that many countries speak of poverty in terms of social exclusion or deprivation. To be poor is often to live on the outskirts of society. The economist and social philosopher Amartya Sen defined poverty in terms of a lack of basic capabilities. According to Sen, poverty implies an overall absence of individual freedom and agency. Individuals in poverty are less able to exert control over their lives. They are more likely to be stigmatized and discriminated against, less likely to be able to take advantage of certain fundamental rights such as voting, plagued by a lower life expectancy, and a host of other constraints.[3]

This introduces the idea that poverty may be more than simply a lack of money. It includes aspects of life that are diminished as a result of an inadequate income.[4] The United Nations has incorporated such a perspective into its definition of poverty for high-economy countries. The organization has included not only a lack of income, but also long-term unemployment, lower life expectancy, and overall rates of illiteracy.[5]

Consequently, there are many ways in which we might define who is poor. Nevertheless, all of these definitions touch on the idea that those in poverty are lacking the basic necessities to maintain a minimally adequate life.

MEASURING POVERTY

In 1964, President Lyndon Johnson historically declared a war on poverty.[6] Delivering his State of the Union address to Congress and the American people, the president announced:

> *This Administration today, here and now, declares unconditional war on poverty in America, and I urge this Congress and all Americans to join with me in that effort. It will not be a short or easy struggle, no single weapon or strategy will suffice, but we shall not rest until that war is won. The richest nation on earth can afford to win it. We cannot afford to lose it.[7]*

Yet, as the administration was to learn on both the domestic and foreign battlefields, a country marching off to war must have a credible estimate of the enemy's size and strength. Surprisingly, up until this point in our nation's history we had no official measure of poverty and therefore no statistics on its scope, shape, or changing nature. The task was therefore to come up with a way of measuring how many people in America were poor.

There are several distinctions that can be made when seeking to measure poverty.[8] These include whether to use an absolute versus a relative measure; a pretransfer versus posttransfer measure; income or assets, earnings or consumption; and finally, monthly or yearly time intervals.

Absolute Versus Relative Measures

A first distinction in measuring poverty is between what is known as an absolute measure of poverty versus a relative measure. An absolute measure defines poverty as a household not having a specific amount of income to purchase those goods and services that are necessary for a minimally adequate life. As discussed, these would include food, shelter, transportation, utilities, and so on. An absolute measure of poverty determines how much these items cost annually and, based on that, estimates an overall dollar amount for the year. Households whose total annual income fall below this amount would be counted as poor, while those above this amount would be considered nonpoor.

The assumption is that there is an income floor which can be empirically calculated, and that living below that floor constitutes poverty. In this sense, such a measure is considered absolute: There is an absolute amount drawn dividing the poor from the nonpoor, with an amount below that line representing material hardship.

On the other hand, a relative measure of poverty looks at where a household's income falls relative to the rest of the population. One relative measure of poverty would be to consider the poor as falling into the bottom 20% or 10% of the income distribution. Another relative measure, widely used throughout the European Union, is to consider those in poverty as having incomes below 50% of a country's median income.[9] Therefore, if median income was $60,000, than those earning less than $30,000 would be counted as poor. If median income were to rise to $70,000, then those below $35,000 would be considered in poverty.

Underlying this type of measure is the concept of relative deprivation. Individuals are considered poor not necessarily because they fall below a particular set amount of income, but rather by the fact that they fall at the bottom of the income distribution. One major advantage of a relative measure, such as falling below 50% of median income, is that it allows us to more easily make comparisons across countries with respect to the extent and depth of poverty.

Pretransfer Versus Posttransfer Measures

A second important distinction in measuring poverty is what is known as a pretransfer versus a posttransfer measure of poverty. A pretransfer measure of poverty relies on a household's overall annual income, but excludes any cash, in-kind benefits, or tax credits that they might receive from the government. On the other hand, a posttransfer measure of poverty includes personal earnings along with government cash programs (e.g., Social Security or unemployment insurance) and/or in-kind programs (e.g., food stamps), as well as tax credits received, in calculating a household's overall income.

Policy analysts will often compare the difference in poverty rates between a pretransfer and posttransfer measure as a way of gauging the impact that government programs have on reducing poverty. A posttransfer measure of poverty will always be lower than a pretransfer measure. How much lower varies widely across countries.

Income Versus Asset-Based Measures

A third important distinction to be made in measuring poverty, is the difference between using income or assets as the measuring stick to determine whether or not a family is considered in poverty. The standard economic approach has been to use a household's income to determine whether or not they fall into poverty. It is through income that households are able to purchase those goods and services necessary for a minimally adequate lifestyle. Such a measure, however, does not take into account the value of any assets that the household may hold.

On the other hand, an asset-based measure of poverty gets at the idea of whether individuals have enough assets (i.e., savings and checking accounts) to allow them to get over a period where their stream of income has been stopped. The concept here is one of protection from a rainy day. This type of measure often defines asset poverty as not having enough liquid assets to keep a household above the poverty line for 3 months.[10]

Earnings Versus Consumption Measures

A fourth distinction that can be made regarding measuring poverty centers on whether to use earnings or consumption as the indicator of how well an individual or household is doing. Most analysts rely on earnings, which are typically measured through income.

However, some have argued that a lack of consumption may be a better indicator of economic and material deprivation.[11] For example, if very little is spent on food, housing, and other necessities, the argument is that such a household is in all likelihood in dire economic straits. One of the problems with using consumption as the measuring stick for poverty is that individuals may be choosing to consume less. In addition, consumption data on a national level are typically quite hard to come by.

Yearly Versus Monthly Measures

A final consideration in measuring poverty has to do with the amount of time under consideration. Most common is to calculate a household's income over the course of a year, and based on that amount, determine whether or not the household fell into poverty. This is what is known as an annual or yearly measure of poverty.

Alternatively, one might measure poverty using a shorter (or longer) span of time. For example, if monthly income data are available, one could determine if a household fell into poverty during any month of the year.[12] Although not as common as an annual measure, a monthly measure has the advantage of detecting specific periods during a year when a household may be experiencing economic troubles. An annual measure is unable to detect such fluctuations.

HOW THE OFFICIAL POVERTY MEASURE
IS CONSTRUCTED

All of these approaches have been, and continue to be, discussed in policy circles.[13] At the time of President Johnson's declared war on poverty, any one of these approaches could have been taken to assess the federal government's efforts. The task fell on an economist working for the Social Security Administration—Molly Orshansky—to devise the country's yardstick for measuring poverty.[14]

The method that Orshansky took was consistent with Adam Smith's definition 200 years earlier. That is, poverty was conceptualized as a failure to have the income necessary to purchase a basic basket of goods and services that allows for a minimally decent level of existence. The approach was therefore absolute rather than relative.

The way that this was (and still largely is) calculated is straightforward. One begins by estimating the household cost of obtaining a minimally adequate diet during the course of the year. For example, in 2021 a family of three would need to spend $7,186.33 to purchase such a diet. This figure is then multiplied by three (in the above case $7,186.33 * 3 = $21,559), which constitutes the official poverty line for a family of three. The reason for using three as a multiplier is that Orshansky relied on a 1955 Department of Agriculture survey showing that families with three or more persons spent approximately one-third of their income on food and the remaining two-thirds on other items, such as clothing, housing, heating, and so on. Thus, the logic in the above example is that if $7,186.33 will purchase a subsistence diet for a family of three, then the remaining $14,372.67 should provide enough income to purchase the other basic necessities needed for a minimally acceptable level of existence.

Several issues are important to point out regarding the official measurement of poverty. First, each year the poverty levels are adjusted to take inflation into account. Obviously, it costs more to purchase that basic basket of goods today than it did 60 years ago. The poverty thresholds are therefore raised each year to reflect the overall increase in the cost of living.

Second, the measuring stick to determine whether individuals fall above or below the poverty threshold is household income. Household income is based on the annual income from all members in the household, calculated from pretax dollars, and does not include in-kind program benefits such as Medicaid or the Supplemental Nutrition Assistance Program or tax credits such as the Earned Income Tax Credit. It does include government cash programs such as Social Security.

Third, the actual estimates of how many Americans fall below the poverty line are derived from the annual Current Population Survey of approximately 60,000 households conducted by the U.S. Bureau of the Census each March. In this survey, households are asked to report their total income for the prior year. That includes all sources of income for each member of the household.

Fourth, the levels of poverty established each year are for the entire nation, and they do not differentiate between the cost of living differences found in various parts of the country. Consequently, there are significant differences across the United States in living costs that are not factored in to the official poverty measure. Trying to survive at the poverty threshold of $21,559 for a family of three in Des Moines, Iowa, will obviously be a different experience from trying to survive on that amount in New York City or San Francisco.[15]

Finally, the monetary amount necessary for a small household's basic needs differs from that of a larger household, and therefore the official poverty levels are adjusted for household size. For example, in 2021 the poverty level for a household of one was $13,788, while that of a household of nine or more was $56,325.[16]

In Table 2.1, we can see the percentage of the U.S. population experiencing various levels of poverty. Three different levels are shown: the official poverty measure (1.00 poverty), poverty and near poverty (below 150% of the official poverty line), and extreme poverty (below 50% of the official poverty line). For 2021, 11.6% of the population fell below the official poverty line, representing 37.9 million individuals; 19.4% experienced poverty or near poverty; and 5.5% were living in extreme poverty.

Table 2.1 PERCENTAGE AND NUMBER OF THE U.S. POPULATION IN POVERTY

Level of Poverty	Percentage	Number (in millions)
	Official Poverty Measure	
0.50 poverty	5.5%	18.2
1.00 poverty	11.6%	37.9
1.50 poverty	19.4%	63.8
	Supplemental Poverty Measure	
0.50 poverty	2.9%	9.5
1.00 poverty	7.8%	25.6
1.50 poverty	19.4%	63.7

SOURCE: U.S. Census Bureau, 2022.

In addition to the official measure of poverty, the Census Bureau has developed an alternative measure of poverty, called the Supplemental Poverty Measure.[17] This is intended to refine the official poverty measure by taking into account a wider variety of expenditures, adjusting for cost-of-living differences, and including noncash benefits along with received tax credits in determining income.[18] The estimates of poverty using the Supplemental Poverty Measure tend to be slightly higher than when using the official measure of poverty (although for 2021 they were lower). In addition, poverty rates for children tend to be lower than the official measure, while poverty rates for those 65 and over are substantially higher.

In the bottom panel of Table 2.1, the extent of poverty in the United States using the Supplemental Poverty Measure is shown. According to this measure, 7.8% of the population fell into poverty in 2021, representing 25.6 million Americans. Furthermore, 19.4% of Americans were in poverty or near poverty, while 2.9% experienced extreme poverty.

DYNAMICS OF POVERTY

As noted, when President Johnson declared a war on poverty in 1964, there was a need to create an overall measure of poverty. As a result, a poverty

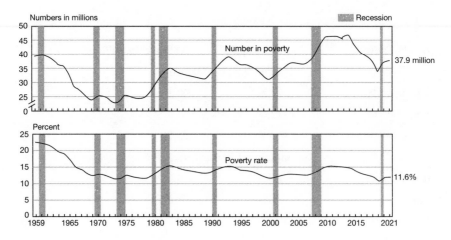

Figure 2.1 Rates of poverty, 1959 to 2021.
SOURCE: U.S. Census Bureau, 2022.

line was established that determined how many people in the United States were in poverty in any given year. The measure was then backdated to 1959, which is why official statistics always begin with that year.

In Figure 2.1, we can see how the overall official poverty rates have changed over the period of 60 plus years from 1959 to 2021. The top panel displays the number of Americans falling into poverty, while the bottom panel shows the poverty rates. Focusing on the rates, several patterns are apparent. From 1959 to 1973, overall poverty in the United States was cut in half. In 1959, the poverty rate stood at 22.4%, and by 1973 it had fallen to 11.1%. Therefore, across a fairly short period of time, the overall rate of poverty was substantially reduced.

We can also see that since the early 1970s, poverty has varied between 10% and 15%. It has tended to go up during periods of recessions (e.g., the early 1980s and 2008–2010) and has declined during periods of economic growth (e.g., the later 1990s and 2010s).

Before the advent of large longitudinal data sets tracking the same people and households over long periods of time, it was often assumed that those who were in poverty at any year were roughly the same people who were in poverty the preceding year and the next year. These assumptions were primarily based on anecdotal evidence. However, beginning in the mid-1970s, social scientists acquired substantial information from large panel data sets (following the same people over time) about the actual patterns and length of time that individuals find themselves in poverty.[19] It turns out that a much more accurate picture is that poverty spells tend to be short but frequent. Poverty is typically fluid rather than the static image often portrayed.

One way of seeing the relatively short-term nature of poverty spells is through a U.S. Census analysis of monthly poverty. Using a large longitudinal data set known as the SIPP (Survey of Income and Program Participation), poverty can be analyzed on a monthly rather than an annual basis. During the 36 months of 2017 through 2019, 27.1% of the U.S. population experienced poverty at some point (defined as being in poverty for two or more consecutive months). Thus, the reach of poverty is quite wide.

However, for those experiencing poverty, the grip of poverty tends to be relatively weak. Table 2.2 displays the percentage of new poverty spells in the United States that end after a given number of months. It turns out

Table 2.2 SPELL LENGTH DISTRIBUTION FOR NEW POVERTY SPELLS

Months in Poverty	Percentage of New Spells Ending
4	18.8%
8	39.3%
12	53.7%
16	72.2%
20	76.8%
24	80.8%
28	84.2%
32	85.8%
36	87.5%
40	87.7%
44	88.0%
48	88.0%

SOURCE: U.S. Census Bureau, 2021.

that after 1 or 2 years a clear majority of people have escaped from poverty. Within 12 months, 53.7% of new spells have ended, while 80.8% have ended after 24 months. Only 12.0% of poverty spells will last more than 48 months.[20] If we consider long-term poverty as four or more consecutive years, then the vast majority of American poverty spells do not meet such a standard. As Mary Jo Bane and David Ellwood explained years ago in one of the first analyses of American poverty spells: "Most people who slip into poverty are quite successful in getting out."[21]

Research has also shown that the reasons for entering and exiting poverty are most often caused by changes in employment status and/or financial resources.[22] As individuals lose jobs or have their hours cut back, the likelihood of poverty increases. Other causes of entrances/exits include changes in family structure (e.g., childbirth or a child leaving home to start their own household) and health-related issues. These are common events that many will experience over the life course. However, some Americans live closer to the poverty line than others, making these events more economically consequential in their lives.

Poverty spells caused by moving out of one's parents' house tend to be the shortest, while spells triggered by the birth of a child tend to be the longest. Employment, education, marriage, and good health are helpful in avoiding poverty along with exiting faster if one does become poor, as well as avoiding multiple spells. Persons of color, women, those in a single-parent household, those with low educational attainment, and individuals with disabilities are at higher risk of new spells, multiple spells, and longer-lasting spells.[23]

Data on time spent on government assistance in terms of the social safety net are also useful to this discussion. A little over a quarter (27.1%) of Americans utilize at least one major means-tested program (Medicaid, the Supplemental Nutrition Program or SNAP, housing assistance, the Supplemental Security Income or SSI program, the Temporary Assistance for Needy Families or TANF program, and/or general assistance) at some point during the year, with an average of 21% participating in at least one program each month.[24]

The length of time spent on welfare programs tends to be short. In one of the first analyses of welfare spells, it was found that most individuals starting a spell of welfare were off the programs after a few years. For those receiving Medicaid, food stamps, or Aid to Families With Dependent Children (AFDC), 54.7% had left after 1 year, 69.4% after 2 years, and 77.4% after 3 years.[25] Yet as with poverty, individuals at some point may return for an additional spell of welfare receipt.[26]

The program that Americans most often strongly associate with welfare—TANF—is used much less than other programs (0.3% of the population 18 and over used the program at some point in 2020).[27] Spells on TANF are also very short; half (50.5%) end within 4 months and over three-quarters (79.6%) within a year. It should be noted that TANF is time limited to no more than 60 months across a lifetime, and some states have adopted lower lifetime limits.

While short-term poverty and welfare use is the norm, long-term poverty is nevertheless a concern. Some analyses show that, at any given moment, a majority of the poor are enduring long-term poverty spells. How could this be, if most new poverty spells end within 1 or 2 years? Bane and Ellwood explained with a helpful metaphor:

Consider the situation in a typical hospital. Most of the persons admitted in any year will require only a very short spell of hospitalization. But a few of the newly admitted patients are chronically ill and will have extended stays in the hospital. If we ask what proportion of all admissions are people who are chronically ill, the answer is relatively few. On the other hand, if we ask what fraction of the number of the hospital's beds at any one time are occupied by the chronically ill, the answer is much larger. The reason is simple. Although the chronically ill account for only a small fraction of all admissions, because they stay so long they end up being a sizable part of the hospital population, and they consume a sizable proportion of the hospital's resources.[28]

So while most Americans who find themselves in poverty will be there for only a matter of a few years, persistent poverty is nevertheless quite real. This minority of the poor does indeed present unique challenges to policymakers compared to the majority of short-termers.

The risk of experiencing multiple spells is also a concern. Despite the norm of short spells for most people, slightly over half of those who escape poverty will return for an additional spell within 5 years.[29] In addition, the longer one experiences poverty, the harder it is to escape and the more likely one is to return. While a majority will exit poverty within the first year, the likelihood of escaping begins to decline after that. For those who have been in poverty for 5 years, their likelihood of exit is less than 20%, and for those who have been in poverty for at least 5 years prior to exit, more than two-thirds will return within 5 years.[30]

THE FACE OF POVERTY

In thinking about who specifically in the U.S. population experiences poverty, there are at least two ways of approaching this question. The first is to focus on which groups have a higher or lower rate of poverty compared to the general population. This allows us to easily examine the extent various population characteristics are associated with the risk of poverty.

The second approach looks at the overall poverty population with respect to group composition. This informs us regarding what the face and makeup of poverty look like. Each of these approaches tells us something slightly different about who the poor are.

Consider the example of race. Non-Whites (specifically African Americans, Hispanics, and Native Americans) have much higher rates of poverty than do Whites. However, the majority of the poor are White. How can this be? The answer is that Whites comprise a much larger segment of the overall population; therefore, even though their rate of poverty is lower than non-Whites, they still make up a majority of the poor. Both of these questions are important in understanding the risk and composition of the poverty population.

Demographics

In Table 2.3, we can see how the rate of poverty and the composition of the poor population vary by demographic attributes. It should first be noted that, with respect to race, Hispanic is considered an ethnic rather than a racial category. Consequently, one could self-identify as both White and Hispanic or as Black and Hispanic.

For Whites (not of Hispanic origin), the poverty rate in 2021 was 8.1%. In contrast, the rate for other racial/ethnic groups was considerably higher. The Black poverty rate was 19.5%; for Hispanics, 17.1%; for Native Americans, 24.3%; while for Asians and Pacific Islanders, 9.3%.

These differences reflect the disparities found across many economic measures. They include significant racial and ethnic differences in income, unemployment rates, net worth, educational attainment, and occupational status.[31] The result is a much higher overall rate of poverty for non-Whites when compared to Whites.[32]

On the other hand, we can also see that approximately two-thirds of the poor self-identify as White. As noted, this is primarily the result of the relatively larger size of the overall White population, so that while the face of poverty is largely White, the risk of poverty is much greater for non-Whites.

Turning to age, the groups most at risk of poverty are children and young adults. Very young children are at a particularly high risk. The poverty rate for children under the age of 5 is 16.5%. Those who are in their prime earning years (mid-30s to mid-50s) tend to have the smallest risk of poverty. This makes perfect sense in that this period of life represents the time in life when individuals tend to be earning the most from their jobs. Approximately 40% of those in poverty are under the age of 25, and an additional 15.3% are age 65 and older.

Women are more likely to experience poverty than men. As with racial differences, this reflects gender differences across a wide range of key economic measures. Household structure, combined with gender, is also strongly related to the risk of poverty. Married couple households have an overall poverty rate of 5.2%, while female-headed households (headed by

Table 2.3 POVERTY RATES AND DEMOGRAPHIC COMPOSITION OF THE POOR

Demographics	Poverty Rate	Percentage of Poor Population
Total	11.6%	100.0%
Race and Ethnicity		
White	10.0%	66.4%
Not of Hispanic origin	8.1%	42.1%
Black	19.5%	22.9%
Asian and Pacific Islander	9.3%	5.1%
Native American	24.3%	2.7%
Hispanic	17.1%	28.5%
Age		
Under 5 years	16.5%	8.0%
5 to 17 years	14.9%	21.4%
18 to 24 years	14.3%	11.0%
25 to 34 years	11.1%	13.0%
35 to 44 years	9.6%	10.9%
45 to 54 years	8.2%	8.7%
55 to 59 years	9.8%	5.4%
60 to 64 years	11.2%	6.3%
65 to 74 years	9.6%	8.6%
75 years and over	11.3%	6.7%
Gender		
Female	12.6%	55.1%
Male	10.5%	44.9%
Household Structure		
Married couple	5.2%	26.8%
Female headed	25.3%	32.3%
Male headed	12.7%	7.0%
Single female	21.7%	18.2%
Single male	17.8%	14.8%

SOURCE: U.S. Census Bureau, 2022.

a woman, usually with children) have a poverty rate of 25.3%; households comprising a single female have a poverty rate of 21.7%.

Consequently, we can see that certain demographic characteristics are closely associated with an elevated risk of poverty. These characteristics have been consistently correlated with poverty over many decades.

Human Capital

A second group of characteristics strongly related to the risk of poverty are what economists label human capital. As discussed in the next chapter, human capital refers to those attributes that individuals have acquired that allow them to compete more effectively in the labor market. These would include the level, quality, and type of acquired education; various skills and talents; job experience; and others. We can also think of human capital as including those attributes that may help or hinder an individual's ability to compete in the labor market, such as having a physical or mental disability.

In Table 2.4 the impact of three specific components of human capital is shown. First, greater levels of education are clearly related to a lowered risk of poverty. Those who have not graduated from high school have a poverty rate of 27.2%. The poverty rate for high school graduates falls to 13.2%, while those with some college have a poverty rate of 9.2%. Finally, college graduates have an overall poverty rate of 4.1%. Considerable research has shown that greater levels of education are strongly related to greater levels of earned income. This is clearly reflected in the patterns found in Table 2.4. In terms of group composition, three-quarters of those in poverty have a high school degree or higher, with 38% having some amount of college.

Disability status is also strongly related to the risk of poverty. Those between the ages of 18 and 64 with a disability have a poverty rate of 24.9%, while those without a disability have a poverty rate of 9.3%. Clearly having a physical or mental disability makes it more difficult to compete

Table 2.4 POVERTY RATES AND HUMAN CAPITAL COMPOSITION OF THE POOR

Human Capital	Poverty Rate	Percentage of Poor Population
Education (in years; for individuals 25 and over)		
Less than 12	27.2%	23.9%
12	13.2%	37.7%
13 to 15	9.2%	23.1%
16 or more	4.1%	15.3%
Disability Status (25 to 64 years)		
Disability	24.9%	19.1%
No disability	9.3%	80.9%
Work Experience (18 to 64 years)		
Did not work	30.0%	65.7%
Worked part-time	12.2%	24.5%
Worked full-time	1.8%	9.8%

SOURCE: U.S. Census Bureau, 2022.

effectively in the labor market. It may shrink the number of jobs one is competitive for, and/or reduce the number of hours one is able to work.

Finally, whether one is employed or not is strongly related to the risk of poverty. Those not working during the year had a poverty rate of 30.0%, while the poverty rate for those working part-time was 12.2%, and 1.8% for full-time workers.

These three human capital characteristics are strongly related to the risk of poverty. They serve to increase an individual's vulnerability when events happen that can precipitate a fall into poverty.

WHERE THE POOR LIVE

An image of the poor often portrayed in the media and elsewhere is that of non-Whites living in high-poverty, inner-city neighborhoods. It is a picture that reinforces the idea that the poor are somehow different from other Americans, that they reside in their own neighborhoods, far away from the rest of America. As Paul Jargowsky wrote:

> *When poverty is discussed, the mental image that often comes to mind is the inner-city, and particularly high-poverty ghettos and barrios in the largest cities. Many people implicitly assume, incorrectly, that most of the nation's poor can be found in these often troubled neighborhoods.*[33]

It is certainly true that the United States remains highly segregated on the basis of race and, increasingly, class. Inner cities across the country have been plagued by ongoing economic and social problems. As scholars such as William Julius Wilson have researched and written about over the years, many of these areas comprise the "truly disadvantaged."

It is therefore surprising to many people to discover that the vast majority of the poor do not live in high-poverty, inner-city neighborhoods. In fact, only between 10% and 15% of those in poverty do so.

Percentage of the Poor Living in High-Poverty Neighborhoods

Based on data from the U.S. Census Bureau, researchers are able to determine what percentage of the poor live in high-poverty neighborhoods. The Census Bureau allows one to analyze these data at the level of what is known as a "census tract" region. A census tract can be thought of as roughly corresponding to a neighborhood and averages around 4,000 people (or about 1,500 housing units). In a densely populated urban area, this might comprise a 10 by 10 square block area, while in a rural location, a census tract would obviously spread out over a much larger geographical region. High-poverty neighborhoods are frequently defined as census tracts in which 40% or more of the residents are living below the poverty line.

Using this definition, Paul Jargowsky analyzed the percentage of the poor that were living in impoverished neighborhoods.[34] We can see in Table 2.5 these percentages for 1990, 2000, 2010, and 2015. In 1990, 15.5%

Table 2.5 PERCENTAGE OF THE POOR LIVING IN HIGH-POVERTY CENSUS
TRACTS AND THE PERCENTAGE OF OVERALL HIGH-POVERTY CENSUS TRACTS.

Year	Percentage of Poor Living in High-Poverty Census Tracts	Percentage of Overall High-Poverty Census Tracts
1990	15.5%	5.7%
2000	10.3%	3.9%
2010	13.6%	5.6%
2015	11.9%	5.0%

SOURCE: Paul A. Jargowsky, 2019.

NOTE: High-poverty census tracts are defined as census tracts in which 40% or
more of residents have earnings below the official poverty line.

of the poor were residing in high-poverty neighborhoods. That figure
dropped to 10.3% by 2000, rose to 13.6% for 2010, and then fell to 11.9%
for 2015.

The second column shows the percentage of all the census tracts in
the United States that were considered high poverty. In 1990, 5.7% of all
census tracts were counted as high-poverty areas. In 2000, this percentage
was 3.9%; by 2010, it had risen to 5.6% and then fell to 5.0% for 2015.
Consequently, although there has been some fluctuation in the percentage
of the poor living in high-poverty neighborhoods, most individuals in
poverty have not and do not live in such neighborhoods.

In addition, Jargowsky found that high-poverty neighborhoods became
less concentrated during this period of time. He noted:

> *Ironically, the concentration of poverty has become deconcentrated, in*
> *a sense. In 1990 and the years prior to that, most high-poverty census*
> *tracts in a metropolitan area could be found in one or two main*
> *clusters. These huge high-poverty, neighborhoods—such as Bedford-*
> *Stuyvesant, Harlem, the South Side of Chicago, North Philadelphia,*
> *and Watts—have become embedded in the public consciousness as*
> *iconic representations of urban poverty. But in the more recent data,*
> *even though the number of high-poverty census tracts has returned to*

levels comparable to 1990, the individual high-poverty tracts are more decentralized and less clustered.[35]

The overall finding of a minority of the poor living in high-poverty neighborhoods is consistent with the results presented previously—that only a small percentage of those experiencing poverty do so for long, extended periods of time. Certainly it is important to keep the deeply entrenched poor in mind when discussing poverty, but it is equally important to keep in mind that they constitute a relatively small proportion of the entire poverty population.

Suburban Poverty

The words *suburban* and *poverty* are rarely uttered together. Yet it turns out that in terms of sheer numbers, there are now more poor people living in suburban areas of the country than are living in central cities.[36]

Elizabeth Kneebone and Alan Berube have addressed this phenomenon in their book *Confronting Suburban Poverty in America*.[37] They analyzed where the poor were living in 100 of the largest metropolitan areas. Approximately two-thirds of the country's population reside in these 100 urban areas. Suburbs were defined as those municipalities within a metropolitan area beyond the first-named city. For example, the city of St. Louis would be counted as the city in the region, while the surrounding municipalities, such as Ferguson, would be counted as suburban.

In Figure 2.2, we can see that the number of poor residents in suburban areas now outnumbers the poor residents' numbers in city areas. While it is true that poverty rates remain higher in central cities than suburbs, because of the population growth in suburbia over the past 50 years, the actual number of poor people is now greater in suburban neighborhoods. In discussing these changes, the authors observed:

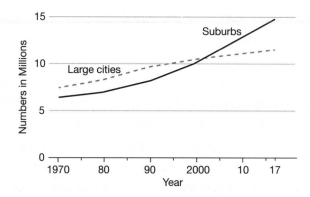

Figure 2.2 Number of poor in suburbs and cities, 1970 to 2017.
SOURCE: Brookings Institution, https://www.brookings.edu/testimonies/the-changing-geography-of-us-poverty.

> *Poverty is a relatively new phenomena in many suburbs. . . . As such, it upends deeply fixed notions of where poverty occurs and whom it affects. As poverty becomes increasingly regional in its scope and reach, it challenges conventional approaches that the nation has taken when dealing with poverty in place. . . . Poverty rates do remain higher in cities and rural communities than elsewhere. But for three decades the poor population has grown in suburbs. The especially rapid pace of growth in the 2000's saw suburbs ultimately outstrip other types of communities so that they now account for the largest poor population in the country.*[38]

Some of this poverty can be found in older, inner-ring suburban areas.[39] These were among the first suburbs developed, often at the beginning of the 20th century. By the end of the 20th century, their infrastructure and housing stock were aging and frequently in need of repair. Likewise, many of these communities saw their school districts deteriorate over time. Consequently, they represent some of the areas where the more affluent have left in order to relocate further afield. The result has been a rising number of poor households in these communities.

Rural Poverty

Like suburban poverty, poverty in rural areas is an unlikely image for many people when asked to describe where the poor live.[40] However, it turns out that the most deeply seated poverty in this country is generally found in rural America. Figure 2.3 shows a map of the most persistently poor counties in the United States over the past 30 years. These are counties that have had poverty rates of 19.5% or higher from the 1990 Census onward.

We can see that the vast majority of these counties are rural or nonmetropolitan.[41] Of the 354 counties with persistent poverty (the total number of counties in the United States is 3,143), over 300 are nonmetropolitan. We can also observe from the map that there are certain distinct regions of the country where these counties are found. Each of these areas has a unique historical legacy of poverty.

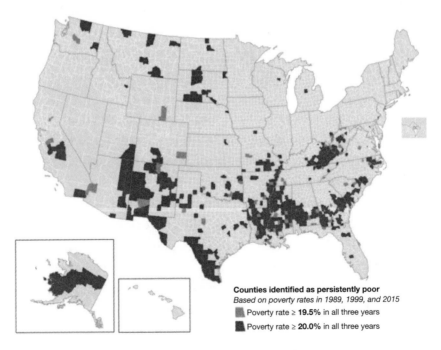

Counties identified as persistently poor
Based on poverty rates in 1989, 1999, and 2015
Poverty rate ≥ **19.5%** in all three years
Poverty rate ≥ **20.0%** in all three years

Figure 2.3 Persistently poor U.S. counties in 1989, 1999, and 2015.
SOURCE: Congressional Research Service.

The area of Appalachia, found predominantly in West Virginia and Kentucky, is a region of long-standing White poverty. It is characterized by the dominance and gradual disappearance of the coal mining industry. As a result, low-paying, service-sector types of jobs are often all that remain.[42]

A second area of long-standing rural poverty can be found across the Deep South and the Mississippi delta region. This is an area with a history of slavery and cotton plantations. Many of the poor in this region are the descendants of slaves and sharecroppers. Again, good job opportunities are often far and few between.[43]

The Texas/Mexican border along the Rio Grande constitutes a third area of deeply entrenched rural poverty. Here one finds a largely Latino population with a long history of being exploited. The presence of colonias along the border represents largely impoverished communities that are lacking basic public services.[44]

The Southwest and northern plains (including parts of Alaska) are also marked by high poverty. Much of this poverty is specific to Native Americans, often on reservations.[45] These counties frequently have some of the highest rates of poverty in the country. The history here is one of exploitation, broken treaties, and the decimation of Native people.

Finally, the central corridor of California represents an area of high poverty, especially among migrant labor. It is a region marked by historically low wages paid to farm laborers and their families. Most of these workers are of Hispanic origin.[46]

The fact that poverty is greater in rural than urban America contradicts the bucolic image that we often have of small towns dotting the countryside. In fact, many of these areas have been crippled by the economic changes that have taken place in the past 50 years.[47] Rural towns have seen their main streets bordered up, and small farming in particular has witnessed devastating changes.

Inner-City Poverty

Poverty is also prevalent in urban, inner cities across the United States. These are areas largely segregated on the basis of race, consisting of African American and Latino populations, often residing in barrios or ghettos. Social policies of the past have largely created these areas through transportation, planning, and zoning laws, as well as discriminatory real estate practices, such as redlining and the denial of home loans on the basis of race. As Jargowsky wrote:

> It is worth noting that those poor living in urban high-poverty areas face significant challenges. Not only must they cope with their own lack of resources, but they reside in neighborhoods that often have low-quality housing stock, vacant buildings, crime and violence, and underperforming schools. Recent research has found significant negative effects on children who grow up in such environments. The existence of these neighborhoods has resulted to a large degree from unwise public policies regarding mortgage lending, exclusionary zoning, and large-scale subsidies for suburban sprawl. While we should improve the social safety net for all poor people, wherever they live, we must also reverse the process that creates economically and racially segregated neighborhoods that make all the problems of poverty worse.[48]

These areas are characterized by a shortage of viable job opportunities. As the economy has shed millions of manufacturing and blue-collar jobs over the past decades, many of the hardest hit areas have been in central cities across the Rust Belt. The result has been rising levels of poverty and unemployment, with residents often unable to escape these conditions as a result of residential segregation.[49] Furthermore, those residing in inner-city poverty-stricken neighborhoods are exposed to a wide range of detrimental social and environmental conditions. These conditions are exacerbated by the isolation and segregated nature of inner cities across the American landscape.

SUMMING UP

What is meant by the term *poverty* can vary depending on the specific context in which it is used. However, most would agree that poverty consists of a lack of necessities to maintain a minimally adequate life. The primary way in which individuals and families are able to acquire these necessities is through income. Therefore, a shortage of income is generally the measuring stick used to determine poverty. In the United States, poverty is officially measured as falling below a particular amount of annual income. This is known as a poverty line or poverty threshold. Households earning less than this amount during the year are counted as poor in the United States.

In any given year, the U.S. poverty rate varies between 10% and 15%. In 2021, the overall rate of poverty was 11.6%, which represented 37.9 million individuals. Most who experience poverty do so for a fairly short amount of time, generally less than 2 or 3 years. However, it is also the case that many individuals will encounter more than one spell of poverty across the span of adulthood.

The other question we have explored in this chapter is what the face of poverty looks like in terms of group makeup. Perhaps the best summary of these data would be that the composition of the poor is diverse. Those in poverty can be found across all geographic regions of the United States. Furthermore, although certain characteristics are associated with an elevated risk of poverty, the face of poverty includes a wide range of demographic and human capital attributes. For example, 38.4% of the poor have attained some level of college education, 26.8% are in married couple families, and 66.4% identify as White.

This brief overview indicates that the experience of poverty is often quite fluid rather than static. Individuals weave in and out of poverty depending on the occurrence of potentially detrimental events such as losing a job. Although there is a small group of households that remain in poverty for an extended period of time, most will find themselves above the poverty threshold as their circumstances improve.

Perspectives on Poverty

Before we explore the structural vulnerability perspective in Chapters 4 through 6, it is helpful to review various approaches that have been utilized for understanding the poverty that we have examined in the last chapter. We begin with a brief overview of what I would label the standard American ideology regarding economic success. This provides a backdrop for then discussing the manner in which many Americans typically understand poverty. Finally, we look at several of the more prominent social science explanations for why poverty exists.

THE AMERICAN IDEOLOGY OF SUCCESS

Since its beginnings, America has prided itself as being a land of opportunity. For the millions of new arrivals coming to its shores, the country represented a new beginning and opportunity. Horace Greeley's famous advice, "Go west, young man" and seek your fortune, illustrated this dream of unlimited opportunity. Such opportunities were viewed as the key building blocks on which individuals and families were able to achieve the American dream.[1] The notion of streets paved with gold, despite its obvious exaggerated implications, reflected this overall idea. Likewise, the image of climbing a ladder of opportunity conveyed the method for achieving such success.

Barbara Jordan, the first Southern Black woman elected to the House of Representative in 1972, expressed this belief well:

It may not be polished, may not be smooth, and it may not be silky, but it is there. I believe that I get from the soil and spirit of Texas the feeling that I, as an individual, can accomplish whatever I want to and that there are no limits, that you can just keep going, just keep soaring. I like that spirit.[2]

As a result of the boundless opportunities found in America, anyone willing to work hard can achieve success. Particularly popular has been the rags-to-riches story.[3] This narrative revolves around individuals beginning their lives in very humble circumstances, but through their hard work, initiative, and skill, eventually accomplish great success in life. By taking full advantage of the opportunities that come their way, they are able to overcome adversity and acquire substantial wealth.

America has long celebrated such individual triumph, in part to demonstrate that literally anything is possible in this land of opportunity. Horatio Alger wrote dozens of stories about young street urchins in the latter part of the 19th century who were able to achieve great success through their hard work and moral character despite having grown up in impoverished conditions. Although Alger's stories were fictional accounts, there have certainly been real-life rags-to-riches stories throughout the course of U.S. history. These examples are provided as proof that if they can do it, so can you. Consequently, a first element of the dominant American ideology has been the belief that the country is blessed with abundant opportunities.

A second premise of the dominant American ideology is the importance placed on individual effort in order to take advantage of these opportunities. America has long emphasized rugged individualism as the way to get ahead in life.[4] In order to take advantage of their opportunities, Americans must be motivated and work hard toward their goals. If they do, success will be theirs: "Hard work is the key to success." It is an adage that we have heard from early childhood onward. "As long as you work hard, you can accomplish almost anything!" one is often told. Americans have been steeped in the ethos of hard work, with those who do so being rewarded with success.

Like the belief in opportunities, the importance of rugged individualism has been stressed since the beginnings of the country. Those seeking to conquer the frontier were seen as needing self-reliance as well as ingenuity and grit to succeed. This emphasis on self-reliance remains today, from the stigma surrounding the use of government safety net programs to the ongoing emphasis on lower taxation. The Protestant work ethic, which has been central to the American identity, has also stressed the importance of rugged individualism and hard work. For example, dedication to work and achievement is often seen as a sign of grace within Protestantism.[5]

Closely connected to these beliefs has been the emphasis on agency—that individuals can control and master their destiny. Agency incorporates the ability to shape the life that one wants to live and to be able to think and act autonomously in pursuit of that desired life. As Jim Cullen noted: "All notions of freedom rest on a sense of agency, the idea that individuals have control over the course of their lives. Agency, in turn, lies at the very core of the American Dream, the bedrock premise upon which all else depends."[6]

Because of the importance placed on rugged individualism and agency, the United States has ensured that various rights and freedoms have been written into law. Beginning with the Bill of Rights up to present-day Supreme Court decisions, a strong emphasis has been placed on protecting the rights and liberties of citizens. As Derek Bok has observed: "Surely there is no other nation where the nature of individual freedom has been elaborated in such detail, or any other society that is so well organized to ensure that essential liberties are defended and preserved."[7]

As a result of the opportunities and freedoms that Americans enjoy, there is also the belief in a level playing field: The rules of the game apply to all, and everyone has a roughly equal chance of succeeding and attaining the American dream.[8] The existence of equality of opportunity ensures that anyone can take advantage of these opportunities in order to do well in their lives.

Finally, because of these beliefs, America has viewed itself as a fair and just society. Given the opportunities available and level playing field, those who succeed economically deserve their rewards. Likewise, those who fail to succeed have only themselves to blame.[9] In this respect, the United States is seen as a meritocracy in which ability and effort are rightfully rewarded.[10]

THE TRADITIONAL PERSPECTIVE ON UNDERSTANDING POVERTY

Given this overall ideology, what has been the traditional approach toward understanding and explaining poverty? There are several key elements that follow from the previous discussion. Poverty has been viewed as largely the result of individual failings and shortcomings. Although there is always a small group of individuals who are understood to not be at fault for their poverty, the vast majority of the poor are responsible for their economic circumstances and are therefore largely undeserving of help or aid. Consequently, government assistance should be kept to a minimum, with strong work incentives emphasized.

Individual Failing

Most notable in this understanding is the emphasis on individual failing as the primary reason for poverty. This takes many different variations: The poor are not working hard enough; have made bad decisions in life; have not acquired necessary skills or education; are not smart or talented enough; have questionable morals; are addicted to alcohol or drugs; and so on. The underlying theme is that the causes of poverty can be understood through the lens of individual failure and pathology.

If we were to ask a random sample of Americans why people are poor, the most likely response would be one that emphasized some aspect of individual failing. Indeed, surveys that have asked this question have found that such factors tend to predominate.[11] Consequently, poverty is explained through individual shortcomings and faults. These include laziness, making poor life decisions, failing to get enough education or job experience, or lack of ability. While these surveys also indicate that structural factors (e.g., the lack of good-paying jobs) are cited, it is the individual deficit reasons that are most often mentioned as important. This should not be surprising in that America has been steeped in the ethos of rugged individualism discussed previously.[12] As a result, individuals are viewed as being in control of their destiny.

Interestingly, even those in poverty often hold these beliefs. For example, in my *Living on the Edge* book, I asked respondents why they were having to use a social welfare program. For the vast majority, they referred to events largely beyond their control, such as losing a job, families splitting up, medical emergencies, and so on. However, when asked why most people were using social welfare programs, their responses were typically along the lines of welfare recipients not working hard enough or making bad decisions in their lives. Such is the power of individual-level explanations.[13]

Attitudes/Motivation/Behavior. The most common individual failure factors surrounding why poverty exists pertain to deficient attitudes, motivation, and/or behavior. The argument is that the poor simply do not have the "right" attitudes necessary to get ahead in life. These include traits such as fortitude and grit, self-responsibility, knowing right from wrong, and so on. The result of these deficiencies is that the poor are not working hard enough to lift themselves out of poverty.

The phrase "Pull yourself up by your own bootstraps" is one embedded in the American lexicon and is often the predominant mindset when it comes to explaining poverty.[14] There is the belief that with hard work and effort, anyone can avoid poverty. George Gilder, in his 1981 book *Wealth and Poverty*, exemplified this:

The only dependable route from poverty is always work, family, and faith. The first principle is that in order to move up, the poor must not only work, they must work harder than the classes above them. Every previous generation of the lower class has made such efforts. But the current poor, white even more than black, are refusing to work hard.[15]

In addition, these negative attitudes are viewed as leading individuals into bad decision-making, which further increases the likelihood of poverty. As Isabel Sawhill argued:

The challenge is to find ways of providing generous support to the poor without disregarding the unpleasant facts about their behavior. Ideally, we need to nudge them toward a different set of behaviors by linking generous governmental assistance to staying in school, delaying child-bearing, getting married, and working full-time. What areas of behavior are we talking about? As I have suggested, three are critical. The first is education; the second is family formation; and the third is work. These have always been the sources of upward mobility in advanced democracies. Those who graduate from high school, wait until marriage to have children, limit the size of their families, and work full-time will not be poor.[16]

From this perspective, the United States is endowed with abundant opportunities for all who are willing to work for them. The way to avoid poverty is to exert oneself through hard work, to make responsible decisions as one goes through life, and to take advantage of the opportunities that are available. Doing so will ensure economic prosperity and will allow individuals to climb the ladder of success.[17]

Cognitive Ability and Talent. A second variation on individual failings emphasizes innate ability and talent. A particular version of this argument is that those experiencing poverty are lacking in intelligence and cognitive ability. This was the approach taken in the controversial book by Richard Herrnstein and Charles Murray, *The Bell Curve*.[18] The authors argued that although both social class and cognitive ability are important for economic success, cognitive ability or intelligence is much more important. Accordingly, those experiencing poverty are more likely to lack intelligence. For example, Herrnstein and Murray described single women with children in the following way:

> *The smarter the woman is, the more likely she will be able to find a job, the more likely she will be able to line up other sources of support (from parents or the father of the child), and the more farsighted she is likely to be about the dangers of going on welfare. Even within the population of women who go on welfare, cognitive ability will vary, and the smarter ones will be better able to get off.*[19]

Another variation of this argument is that those in poverty are lacking in innate abilities, skills, and talents. These are viewed as the attributes that allow one to get ahead in life. As a result, such individuals are unable to compete effectively in the labor market and are therefore more prone to experiencing poverty.

The Deserving and Undeserving Poor

Closely connected to individual failing has been the concept of deservedness.[20] This criterion has been used for centuries, particularly since the English Poor Laws of 1601, to divide the poor into the categories of deserving and undeserving. The deserving poor are those deemed worthy of our compassion and assistance because they find themselves in poverty through little fault of their own. As a result, an injustice has occurred. Such persons would include those who have suffered from an unavoidable illness or accident, children, widows, and so on.

On the other hand, individuals falling into the undeserving poor category are seen as meriting neither our compassion nor our assistance. As discussed previously, such poverty is perceived as brought on by a lack of initiative, laziness, bad decisions, or some other failing, and therefore impoverishment is a just and fair consequence of prior behavior.

Within the United States, the vast majority of the poor are seen as falling into the undeserving category and are frequently referred to as the able-bodied poor. As such, they have no one to blame but themselves. Given the abundance of opportunities, they need to simply, as many would say, "Get a job!"

To some extent this perspective has been applied in the United States even to children and the elderly, groups that are often considered deserving of help. While a child cannot be held responsible for their poverty, their parents certainly can be. This is particularly the case for single parents. Bad decision-making on the part of such parents has put their children at risk of poverty, and the parents themselves should be held accountable.[21] Similarly, seniors in poverty can be faulted for failing to plan and save enough during their working years for retirement.

On the other hand, a small segment of the poverty population is considered deserving of compassion and assistance. For these individuals, poverty is understood to be largely unavoidable. Examples of the deserving poor might include those who have suffered from a catastrophic accident or from an illness beyond their control. In these cases, help from social programs is warranted.

Sense of Shame

As argued, the traditional understanding of poverty has been one of individual shortcomings and moral failing, with an overall disdain of the poor by the general population. The result is that the impoverished should be ashamed to find themselves in poverty.[22] This sense of shame is reflected in the design and punitive nature of the social safety net in the United States.[23]

Research has shown that considerable stigma is attached to being poor, particularly to using social welfare programs. Robert Walker wrote:

Shaming that is backed by the power of the state becomes stigmatization. People in poverty are stigmatized in political discourse by being considered a problem while policies that are put in place specifically to address poverty are likely to be stigmatizing. People in poverty are liable to feel ashamed of their circumstances, including the receipt of stigmatizing welfare benefits, and may well be discriminated against as a result of receiving benefits and during the process of claiming them.[24]

In interviews for my *Living on the Edge* book, welfare recipients repeatedly mentioned that they felt this stigma on a daily basis. From using food stamps in the grocery store, to feelings of being constantly watched and scrutinized. For example, a 29-year-old mother described her acute awareness of being sized up by front-line workers in the medical field:

Some receptionists turn off the friendliness when they see Medical Assistance. Sometimes I catch them looking at me, maybe if I have on a necklace or something. I don't think I look like the stereotypical welfare mother, and I see them scrutinizing me and thinking it over. It's pretty subtle.[25]

One major reason for the ongoing stigmatization and shaming of the poor and welfare recipients is to make their current condition as uncomfortable as possible in order that they will want to work their way out of poverty. The result is that safety net programs are hard to apply for, provide meager benefits, and make it difficult to remain on.[26] All of this is designed to reflect the sense of shame and discomfort that those in poverty should feel.

Poverty Is Primarily Just

Based on the preceding premises, although poverty might be considered regrettable, it is nevertheless considered both fair and justifiable. For most who find themselves in poverty, they have no one but themselves to blame. Their current economic condition is the result of their prior behavior. In this sense, there is a balance between past and present outcomes, implying that justice is being served.

As I have argued in other work, most theories of justice are premised on this notion of balance.[27] When prior actions and future outcomes are roughly in balance with one another, the world is viewed as fair or just. Consequently, economic success or failure should be determined by prior actions and behaviors.

The result of this is that the status quo of poverty amid plenty is viewed as acceptable. As a result, there is a general lack of motivation to address or alleviate poverty within the overall population. Likewise, no major government intervention is warranted. Because those in poverty are re-sponsible for their circumstances, a social safety net should be kept to a minimum. In fact, a generous social welfare state is viewed as creating dependency, further entrapping those in poverty. Such has been the long-standing conservative argument against welfare programs.[28]

SOCIAL SCIENCE APPROACHES
TO UNDERSTANDING POVERTY

In contrast with the traditional or common-sense perspective on poverty, social science approaches to understanding poverty are generally based on an array of research conducted in the various academic disciplines. These include sociology, economics, anthropology, and political science. In this section, I review several of the more prominent explanations of poverty coming out of these disciplines.

Marxist Critiques of Capitalism

A very influential structural critique of capitalism can be found in the writings of Karl Marx. Marx was researching and writing during the middle and later part of the 19th century. Considerable political and ec-onomic turmoil was occurring in Europe during this period. Much of Marx's work focused on attempting to answer two broad questions. First, what has been the dynamic that has driven societal change across time?

Second, how might we better understand the manner in which exploitation occurs within capitalism?

According to Marx, history can be seen as an ongoing conflict between two broad classes in society: those who Marx called the owners of the means of production and the rest of society. The means of production refers to those goods or commodities capable of generating or reproducing greater wealth. In today's society, they would include factories, intellectual property, real estate, and so on. There is an inherent antagonism and conflict between these two classes. In ancient societies this was represented by the master/slave; in feudal times, the lord/serf; under capitalism, the bourgeoisie/proletariat. This conflict eventually leads to a broad economic and societal transformation.

Much of Marx's writing was concerned with capitalist societies and the exploitative class relations found within them. In feudal times, workers had produced their own goods and bartered or sold them. Capitalism brought about a dramatic change—people began to work in settings other than the home (i.e., a factory). Furthermore, they worked not for themselves but for the capitalists who owned the factories and paid workers a wage in return for their labor.

Competition is inherent within capitalism. In order for capitalists to remain competitive and profitable in the economic marketplace, they must try to keep the costs of their products low. In order to do so, there is pressure to pay their employees as low a wage as possible. This pressure also encourages technological developments to replace labor, such as automation or computerization, or locating labor to other parts of the globe where wages might be significantly lower.

Marx argued that workers are not paid at rates that reflect the true value of what they produce. The difference between what they are paid and what the product is actually worth—Marx called this the surplus value—is what the capitalists take for their own profit. This, according to Marx, represents the exploitation of workers by capitalists. It is in the nature of capitalism for the owners of the means of production to increase profits at the workers' expense:

What then, is the general law which determines the rise and fall of wages and profit in their reciprocal relation? They stand in inverse ratio to each other. Capital's share, profit, rises in the same proportion as labour's share, wages, falls, and vice versa. Profit rises to the extent that wages fall; it falls to the extent that wages rise.[29]

As capitalism develops, it brings about a greater division of labor, which allows the capitalist to produce more goods with fewer workers, resulting in even greater profits. Many of the remaining jobs become increasingly simplified, requiring fewer skills. This, in turn, makes individual workers more expendable, driving wages down even further.

With a decreased need for workers and easily replaceable labor, more individuals are reduced to what Marx called the industrial reserve army. The soldiers in this army live much of their lives in or near poverty and are able to work and fully support themselves only during periods of boom or economic expansion. As Marx wrote: "Thus the forest of uplifted arms demanding work becomes ever thicker, while the arms themselves become ever thinner."[30]

According to Marx, then, poverty is simply inherent in the economic structure of capitalism: It is an inevitable byproduct of the exploitation of workers by capitalists. As capitalism further develops, it will leave in its wake more and more individuals and families that are on, or have fallen over, the economic precipice.[31]

Human Capital

In contrast to the Marxist critique of capitalism, human capital theory argues that poverty is the result of individuals lacking what economists refer to as human capital. Human capital represents that basket of acquired skills and experiences that allow individuals to compete in the labor market. These would include the quantity and quality of education one has received, job experience and training, skills developed, good health, and so on.

The labor market is conceptualized as a competitive system in which wages are determined by supply and demand as well as the resources or human capital that people possess. Those who do well in the labor market do so primarily as a result of the human capital they have acquired. Such people are in greater demand and hence enjoy brighter job prospects. Those experiencing poverty tend to be lacking in human capital and therefore cannot compete as effectively in the labor market. And in fact, research has shown that those with greater human capital will generally do better economically than those with less human capital (as I discuss in the next chapter).[32]

According to this perspective, the way to reduce poverty is to concentrate on upgrading individual skills. This might include ensuring graduating from high school, teaching people marketable trades, enabling them to acquire job experience, and so on. This premise underlies most job training programs directed at the poor.[33]

Dual Labor Market Theory

The dual labor market theory arose as a reaction against the perceived failings of the human capital theory. Whereas human capital assumes that there is one labor market in operation, the dual labor market perspective posits the existence of two quite distinct markets that operate according to different rules.[34] In the primary market, jobs are characterized by stability, high wages and benefits, and good working conditions. This market is limited to a certain sector of the private economy, called the core or monopoly sector. Firms within the monopoly sector tend to be large and capital intensive and to possess sizable and often international markets (e.g., the automobile industry, pharmaceuticals, etc.). Within such firms, there exists what is called an internal labor market. Individuals from the outside can only enter this internal labor market at certain points, often the bottom rung of a career ladder. Jobs higher up the ladder are filled within the firm through promotion.

On the other hand, jobs in the secondary labor market are characterized as menial, having poor working conditions, low wages, little stability, and few benefits. The secondary market exists primarily within what is called the peripheral or competitive sector of the private economy. Firms within the competitive sector tend to be small and labor intensive, with lower productivity per worker and more local markets. In addition, an individual's labor and skills can be easily replaced by another individual's. Examples include restaurants, retail sales, custodial work, landscaping, and so on.

The determinants of earnings vary between markets. In the primary market, earnings are determined by the worker's position in the career structure as well as seniority. In contrast, wages in the secondary labor market are largely determined by market forces. Since workers in this market are generally considered homogeneous and have little union power, their wages are the product of supply and demand. Thus, differences in earnings are due primarily to the number of hours worked.

The dual labor market approach seeks to explain the persistent poverty of different social groups and persistent racial and gender wage differences. It argues that, for a variety of reasons (e.g., statistical discrimination, fewer skills, employers' perceptions of a lack of worker commitment), women and minorities are more likely to begin their work careers in the secondary labor market. As Randy Hodson and Robert Kaufman noted: "Once workers enter the secondary market, they acquire unstable work histories."[35] Employers in the primary labor market then use these histories as evidence that they are inadequate workers, and thus they are blocked from moving into the primary market. This in turn helps to perpetuate income inequality and poverty.

People are poor not because they do not participate in the economy but because of the way in which they participate in the economy. Because of the instability and low wages in the secondary labor market, workers in such jobs experience occasional unemployment and may turn to the social safety net in order to survive lean times. Individuals in these jobs routinely face economic insecurity and hardship, with poverty a frequent companion.

Functionalism

Functionalism has a long history in the social sciences. Its origins began at the end of the 19th and early 20th centuries as European anthropologists traveled to non-Western cultures such as those in the Pacific Islands. There they observed cultural adaptations and traits that, at first glance, were hard to understand from a Western European lens. However, after immersing themselves in these cultures, they realized that such traits and adaptations served a number of purposes for specific groups and for the society as a whole. Out of this ethnographic work arose the perspective known as structural functionalism.

The sociologist Robert Merton defined functions as "those observed consequences which make for the adaptation or adjustment of a given system; and dysfunctions, those observed consequences which lessen the adaptation or adjustment of the system."[36] Functions can be both intended (manifested functions) and unintended (latent functions). For an institution or phenomenon to survive in a society, it must somehow be functional for that society. If it is not, it eventually disappears or is modified.

Using this perspective, Herbert Gans sought to explain the persistence of poverty in the United States.[37] He began his argument by stating that the reason poverty has remained at high levels is because it must be serving a number of important functions for society in general, and specifically, it serves important economic, social, and political functions for the well to do. Although this may at first seem counterintuitive, Gans went on to detail a number of potential functions that are served by the presence of poverty. For example, the existence of poverty ensures that undesirable, low-wage work gets done. Because those in poverty have few job alternatives, they are forced to take these undesirable but necessary jobs. Poverty also creates a number of occupations and professions that serve and rely on the poor (i.e., academics writing books about poverty). Or that the poor can be identified and punished as deviants (e.g., welfare freeloaders) by political actors in order to uphold the legitimacy of dominant norms and to further their own political careers. He concluded:

My analysis suggests that the alternatives for poverty are themselves dysfunctional for the affluent population, and it ultimately comes to a conclusion which is not very different from that of radical sociologists. To wit: that social phenomena which are functional for affluent groups and dysfunctional for poor ones persist; that when the elimination of such phenomena through functional alternatives generates dysfunctions for the affluent, they will continue to persist; and that phenomena like poverty can be eliminated only when they either become sufficiently dysfunctional for the affluent or when the poor can obtain enough power to change the system of social stratification.[38]

Some have also argued that the social safety net itself is functional for society, not because it provides help to the needy, but because it placates and regulates the poor.[39] As Carol Stack argued:

It is clear that mere reform of existing programs can never be expected to eliminate an impoverished class in America. The effect of such programs is that they maintain the existence of such a class. Welfare programs merely act as flexible mechanisms to alleviate the more obvious symptoms of poverty while inching forward just enough to purchase acquiescence and silence on the part of the members of this class and their liberal supporters. . . . These programs are not merely passive victims of underfunding and conservative obstructionism. In fact they are active purveyors of the status quo, staunch defenders of the economic imperative that demands maintenance of a sizable but docile impoverished class.[40]

Such analysts pointed out that safety net programs tend to expand during times of social upheaval precisely for this reason. For example, the beginnings of the modern welfare state in the United States can be traced back to the Social Security Act of 1935. This act was signed into law at a time when the country was in its deepest depression, and food riots were occurring on the streets. Likewise, the War on Poverty initiatives that began in the mid-1960s also occurred at a time of tremendous turmoil and unrest. From this perspective, the welfare state is designed to placate the poor so that they are not so desperate they revolt against the government and status quo.

Distribution of Welfare State Resources

The distribution of welfare state resource theory argues that a primary reason for poverty has to do with a lack of political and policy support toward the poor. The focus is on variation in poverty rates across countries. The argument is that lower poverty rates are the result of more generous and effective social welfare state programs. As sociologist David Brady explained:

> *What explains this tremendous variation in poverty across the affluent Western democracies? This question represents a serious challenge to any theory of poverty. Theories of poverty should be able to explain why some affluent Western democracies maintain substantial poverty and others are more egalitarian and accomplish low levels of poverty. Yet, the conventional approach in poverty studies is to analyze only the United States and to compare the characteristics of poor people (perhaps in poor neighborhoods) to nonpoor people. It is not an exaggeration to say that the vast majority of poverty studies explain why one group of people within a country are more likely to be poor, or why some individuals are poor while others are not. Thus, conventional poverty research stops short of confronting the enormous cross-national differences.*[41]

Brady went on to argue:

> *In contrast, I contend that these cross-national and historical differences in poverty are principally driven by politics. This book makes the simple claim that the distribution of resources in states and markets is inherently political. I explicitly seek to challenge the mainstream*

view that poverty is an inescapable, if perhaps unfortunate, outcome of an individual's failings or a society's labor markets and demography. Instead, I argue that societies make collective choices about how to divide their resources. These choices are acted upon in the organization and states that govern the societies, and then become institutionalized through the welfare state. Where poverty is low, equality has been institutionalized. Where poverty is widespread, as most visibly demonstrated by the United States, there has been a failure to institutionalize equality.[42]

Poverty rates vary widely by country. The United States is at the high end in terms of the extent and depth of its poverty. From this perspective, the reason lies in its extremely weak and limited social safety net programs. As specific events occur to households that can trigger spells of poverty (e.g., loss of a job, families splitting up, health problems), the programs designed to protect households from poverty come up short. When comparing pretransfer with posttransfer rates of poverty, the United States has the smallest rate of reduction compared to the other Organization for Economic Cooperation and Development countries. As a result, the United States is plagued by high rates of poverty and inequality.

In more recent work, Brady argued that the United States in particular attaches a much higher penalty to specific behaviors.[43] These include single parenthood, unemployment, and low educational attainment. While other countries provide support for those who fall into these categories, U.S. policy has sought to punish individuals in these groups by withholding economic support. The result is a much higher overall rate of poverty.[44]

Culture of Poverty

The culture of poverty thesis arose from the ethnographic work of anthropologist Oscar Lewis. His study *Five Families* examined lower class Mexican family life, while a later work, *La Vida*, focused on Puerto

Rican families residing in slum communities in both New York City and Puerto Rico.[45] Based on these ethnographies, Lewis argued that a culture of poverty existed.

The argument is that individuals and families living in communities that have been mired in long-term poverty develop a way of life that allows them to better cope with their difficult circumstances, but which in turn makes it more difficult to escape from poverty. Lewis wrote that the term *culture of poverty*

> *is the label for a specific conceptual model that describes in positive terms a subculture of Western society with its own structure and rationale, a way of life handed on from generation to generation along family lines. The culture of poverty is not just a matter of deprivation or disorganization, a term signifying the absence of something. It is a culture in the traditional anthropological sense in that it provides human beings with a design for living, with a ready-made set of solutions for human problems, and so serves a significant adaptive function.[46]*

Lewis felt that this way of life applied to only perhaps 20% of those in poverty. He argued that it is found in those areas of long-standing impoverishment, such as rural Appalachia or inner-city, racially segregated ghettos. Lewis wrote:

> *It is both an adaptation and a reaction of the poor to their marginal position in a class-stratified, highly individuated, capitalist society. It represents an effort to cope with feelings of hopelessness and despair that arise from the realization by the members of the marginal communities in these societies of the improbability of their achieving success in terms of the prevailing values and goals.[47]*

Those within this culture are viewed as displaying certain traits and behaviors that reflect the environmental conditions they face. These include having a present-time orientation, feelings of alienation and fatalism, and a greater acceptance of alternative avenues and behaviors for achieving success (e.g., criminal activity, out-of-wedlock births, etc.). Lewis argued that once the culture of poverty has come into existence, it tends to perpetuate itself across generations.

The culture of poverty is understood as a rational response to attempting to survive in an environment plagued by severe poverty. However, while such a culture makes coping with the present more tolerable, it also hinders the ability of individuals to climb out of poverty. For example, although a present-time orientation makes perfect sense for dealing with the daily turmoil of poverty, it works against long-term planning and goal setting, which can facilitate escaping poverty.

More recent uses of the culture of poverty perspective have largely followed in this tradition.[48] Mario Small and colleagues noted: "Culture is back on the poverty research agenda. Over the past decade sociologists, demographers, and even economists have begun asking questions about the role of culture in many aspects of poverty and even explicitly explaining the behavior of the low-income population in reference to cultural factors."[49] In addition, the literature on "poverty traps" largely falls within this tradition as well.[50]

The Social Isolation Explanation

William Julius Wilson offered a somewhat different perspective on the contribution of culture to poverty, noting that the "key theoretical concept is not culture of poverty but social isolation."[51] Wilson's theory is based on an analysis of the increasing problems found within inner cities and the reasons such problems have worsened over the past 50 years. Wilson dealt with a specific group in poverty, those he termed "the truly disadvantaged." He argued that many of the problems found in inner cities today are the result of what he labeled concentration effects: "The social transformation of the inner city has resulted in a disproportionate concentration of the most disadvantaged segments of the urban black population, creating a social milieu significantly different from the environment that existed in these communities several decades ago."[52]

In addition, the inner city has become increasingly isolated from mainstream social behavior. As the Black middle and working classes have left the inner cities, fewer positive role models remained in the community. The inner city has therefore become more socially isolated, while at the same time experiencing a greater concentration of deviant behavior:

> *The communities of the underclass are plagued by massive joblessness, flagrant and open lawlessness, and low-achieving schools, and therefore tend to be avoided by outsiders. Consequently, the residents of these areas, whether women and children of welfare families or aggressive street criminals, have become increasingly socially isolated from mainstream patterns of behavior.*[53]

Wilson repeatedly pointed out that the ultimate cause of inner-city conditions is not the culture itself but rather the social structural constraints and the lack of opportunities. Thus, "the key conclusion from a public policy perspective is that programs created to alleviate poverty, joblessness, and related forms of social dislocation should place primary focus on changing the social and economic situation, not the cultural traits, of the ghetto underclass."[54] Wilson further distinguished his concept of social isolation from that of a culture of poverty by arguing that cultural traits are not self-perpetuating but rather adaptations to structural conditions. When structural conditions change, culture will change along with it. Nevertheless, Wilson emphasized that a distinct culture exists in the inner city, and that this culture helps to maintain poverty. Thus, while it may not be the ultimate factor, it does contribute heavily to Wilson's understanding of poverty.

CONCLUSION

In this chapter we have briefly reviewed various explanations for why poverty exists in the United States. We first examined what I have called the traditional American ideology of economic success and failure, and how it has been applied to understanding poverty. It has been the dominant mindset used to explain and rationalize poverty. Certainly there is a segment of the American population that do not abide by this set of beliefs, but survey data indicate that a significant percentage of Americans do.

This perspective has largely shaped the country's response to poverty. That response has been one of "tough love" and/or neglect. Proactive policies have been kept to a minimum, and those programs that do provide economic assistance are difficult to qualify for and steeped in work incentives.

Social scientists have also provided explanations of poverty. These explanations tend to focus on particular dynamics within society as the causes of poverty. They include patterns of exploitation, culture, social welfare expenditures, and others.

We now turn to an alternative understanding of poverty in the chapters ahead. It is designed to provide new insights into why poverty exists and persists. It has been developed over a number of years and is based on my ongoing research and analysis into the subject, along with the work of many scholars in the field of poverty studies.

PART II

The Structural Vulnerability Framework

4
—

Economic Vulnerability and
the Role of Human Capital

Given the backdrop of the explanations of poverty discussed in the last chapter, how might we better understand the dynamics of poverty and how they play out on a daily basis? The next three chapters describe in detail the structural vulnerability explanation of poverty. As I mentioned in the introductory chapter, this perspective has developed out of my prior work examining the lives of welfare recipients, those in poverty, and the pursuit of the American dream. It provides a framework for understanding who loses out at the economic game, while emphasizing that the game itself is structured in a way that ultimately produces a significant number of economic losers. I draw on this body of work as well as other research in order to articulate the structural vulnerability approach.

There are three basic premises underlying this perspective. The first is that specific characteristics, such as the lack of human capital, tend to place individuals in a vulnerable position when detrimental events and crises occur. The occurrence of these events (e.g., loss of a job, family breakup, ill health) can result in pushing individuals into poverty. In addition, the lack of human capital also increases the likelihood of such events occurring (particularly those related to the labor market). In this sense, human capital characteristics help to explain who in the population is likely to encounter poverty more frequently and for longer periods of time.

Second, the acquisition of such human capital is strongly influenced by the impact that cumulative inequality has on this process. Those who find themselves growing up in a working class or lower income home will face greater odds in terms of acquiring marketable education and skills during their lifetime. The process of cumulative disadvantage or advantage tends to compound over the course of a lifetime. Additional attributes also play a role in the acquisition of human capital, including race, gender, and innate ability.

Finally, while individual characteristics help to explain who loses out at the economic game, economic and political forces on the structural level ensure that there will be losers in the first place. In this sense, the dynamic of poverty can be described as a game of musical chairs in which those with the least advantageous characteristics are likely to find themselves without a chair and therefore left standing with a heightened risk of economic vulnerability. Each of these components is discussed in the upcoming chapters.

ECONOMIC VULNERABILITY AND HUMAN CAPITAL

Essential to an initial understanding of poverty are the concepts of economic vulnerability and the importance of the lack of particular attributes in accentuating such vulnerability. Individuals more likely to experience poverty tend to have attributes that put them at a disadvantage vis-à-vis their earnings ability within the labor market.

As discussed in the prior chapter, these attributes can be thought of largely in terms of what economists refer to as human capital, or that basket of skills, credentials, and qualifications that individuals bring with them into the job market.[1] Those who do well in the labor market often do so as a result of the human capital they have acquired (in particular, they possess marketable skills and experience). As a result, they are in greater demand by employers and will therefore enjoy brighter job and earnings prospects.[2]

On the other hand, those facing an elevated risk of poverty tend to have acquired less valuable human capital. For example, education may be truncated or of an inferior quality, while job experience and skills may be less marketable. This results in individuals being less attractive in the job market. Additional factors can also limit the ability to effectively compete in the labor market. Individuals residing in inner cities or remote rural areas often face diminished job prospects. Single mothers with young children experience reduced flexibility in their ability to take a job as a result of having to arrange child care. Likewise, those with a physical or mental disability may be more limited in terms of the type of jobs and number of hours they may work.

In addition, attributes such as race and gender can result in employers using such characteristics to screen and/or limit the promotion of potential employees. In one of the more blatant examples, sociologist Devah Pager's employment audit experiments found that, despite identical qualifications, White job applicants were much more likely to receive positive employer responses (either a callback or job offer) compared to Black applicants. This was the case even when Whites had a criminal record and identically credentialed African Americans did not (17% positive responses for Whites with a felony conviction compared to 13% for African Americans with a clean record). Pager and her colleagues concluded that: "Our findings add to a large research program demonstrating the continuing contribution of discrimination to racial inequality in the post-civil rights era."[3]

Likewise, gender has been shown to impact the acquisition of human capital.[4] For example, throughout their schooling, girls are more likely to be steered into less lucrative career paths. Gender discrimination in the labor market has also been shown to be prevalent, as demonstrated in numerous research studies and court cases.[5] The labor market remains highly segregated by gender, with women concentrated in lower paying jobs. Women are also more likely than men to face barriers to career advancement and higher earnings. This results in less valuable skills and experience being acquired across the life course.

In short, those experiencing poverty are more likely to have characteristics that place them at a disadvantage in terms of competing in the labor market. This can be clearly seen in the first table. Table 4.1 contains an analysis that my colleague Steve Fazzari and I conducted using the 2020 March Current Population Survey. This is the same survey used to derive the annual estimates of poverty and income in the United States.

The analysis is confined to those between the ages of 25 and 59 (often considered the prime working years) who are in the labor force. This includes both the employed and the unemployed. We divided our sample into eight groups based on their education, race, and gender.

The focus is on the percentage of individuals in each group holding an adequately paying job, defined as having a weekly wage that pays more than twice the poverty threshold for a household of two. This comes out to $663 a week, or approximately $16.50 an hour in 2020 dollars.

What we can see in the first column of Table 4.1 are the differences in holding a decent-paying job across the eight categories. These range from 85.6% (for White males with more than 12 years of education) to 33.7% (for non-White females with 12 or fewer years of education). The effects of education, race, and gender all exert a strong influence on the probabilities of having an adequately paying job.

Table 4.1 LIKELIHOOD OF INDIVIDUALS AGED 25–59 HAVING AN ADEQUATELY PAYING JOB

Characteristics	Percentage	Odds
Beyond high school/White/male	85.6%	12.36
Beyond high school/White/female	76.4%	6.49
Beyond high school/non-White/male	76.3%	6.34
Beyond high school/non-White/female	62.9%	3.33
High school or less/White/male	65.4 %	3.71
High school or less/White/female	49.8%	1.95
High school or less/non-White/male	49.2%	1.90
High school or less/non-White/female	33.7%	1.00

SOURCE: Current Population Survey, Fazzari and Rank calculations.

NOTE: *Adequately paying job* is defined as twice the poverty line for a household of two.

In the second column are the results from a multivariate analysis in which logit models were computed to look at the independent effects of education, race, and gender on the likelihood of holding a decent-paying job. Here we see the relative odds of each group attaining a decent-paying job compared to the reference group of non-White females with 12 or fewer years of education. Again, we find sizable differences across the eight groups. For example, White males with more than 12 years of education were over 12 times more likely to have a good-paying job when compared to non-White females with 12 or fewer years of education.

A further illustration of the effect of human capital on poverty is the association between education and income.[6] There is a strong direct relationship between the amount of education an individual has and their level of income. Table 4.2 shows the strength of this relationship. As individuals acquire more education, they earn more money. Those with less than 12 years of education earn a median of $25,322 a year, $35,315 for those with a high school diploma, while those with 16 or more years of education earn a median of $69,603. Similarly, as we saw in Chapter 2, individuals with lower levels of education are more likely to experience poverty. They range from a high of 27.2% for those without a high school diploma to a low of 4.1% for college graduates. There is clearly a strong relationship between the amount of education an individual has and their risk of poverty. The same can be said for said for other components of human capital, such as skills and experience.[7]

However, these factors alone do not directly cause poverty. If they were solely responsible, how might we explain the fluid movements of people

Table 4.2 INCOME AND POVERTY RATES BY LEVEL OF EDUCATION

Education (Years)	Median Income	Poverty Rate
Less than 12	$25,322	27.2%
12	$35,315	13.2%
13–15	$39,179	9.2%
16 or more	$69,603	4.1%

SOURCE: U.S. Census Bureau, 2022.

in and out of poverty, as indicated by the research into the longitudinal dynamics of poverty discussed in Chapter 2? As we saw previously, the typical pattern is that individuals may be poor for 1 or 2 years and then get themselves above the poverty line, perhaps experiencing an additional spell of poverty in the future. Furthermore, the life course patterns of poverty also indicate the commonality of short but recurring periods of impoverishment (as we will see in Chapter 6). For many people, their personal and human capital characteristics have remained constant while their poverty status has not. An explanation that focuses solely on human capital cannot in and of itself account for such transitions.

What is argued here is that the lack of human capital results in certain life crises occurring more often and with greater intensity. This would appear particularly true for labor market difficulties. Those with less human capital are more likely to experience job instability, longer periods of unemployment, lower wages, and part-time work. Each of these, in turn, is associated with an elevated risk of poverty.

In addition, the lack of human capital places the individual in a more economically vulnerable position when faced with the loss of employment, changes in family status, illness and incapacitation, and so on. Individuals and families who are marginalized in terms of their ability to participate in the free market system will have more difficult times weathering such storms.[8] It will take them longer to find a job or to earn enough to tide them through the breakup of a family or an illness. When such events take place, they can throw individuals into poverty for a period of time until they are able to get back on their feet. It is estimated that 36% of Americans do not have enough liquid assets to cover a $400 emergency.[9] When such an emergency strikes, those who are lacking in human capital can be catastrophically impacted.

A lack of human capital therefore increases the likelihood that particular detrimental economic events will occur, such as not having a job, as well as making it more difficult to weather such events when they do occur. As a result, those who are lacking in human capital might be thought of as walking a very fine line. If nothing out of the ordinary happens, many of these families are able to just get by. However, should a crisis occur such as the loss of a job, an unanticipated medical problem, or a costly but needed repair of an automobile, it often places the household into an economic tailspin.[10]

Many of the families that I interviewed for my book, *Living on the Edge*, were households straddling the borderline between keeping their heads above water and poverty. One wrong step, and they were likely to land back in poverty and on welfare. They simply did not have the resources and assets necessary to tide them over for more than several weeks. For example, I asked Cindy and Jeff Franklin, a married couple with two children, to describe these types of situations:

CINDY: *Well, I think it's running out of money. [Sighs] If something comes up—a car repair or [pause] our refrigerator's on the fritz. . . . We have enough money for a nice, adequate, simple lifestyle as long as nothing happens. If something happens, then we really get thrown in a tizzy. And I'd say that's the worst—that's the worst.*

JEFF: *Yeah, 'cause just recently, in the last month, the car that we had was about to rust apart. Sort of literally. And so we had to switch cars. And my parents had this car that we've got now, sitting around. They gave it to us for free, but we had to put about two hundred dollars into it just to get it in safe enough condition so that we don't have to constantly be wondering if something's gonna break on it.*

CINDY: *I think that sense of having to choose—the car is a real good example of it—having to choose between letting things go—in a situation that's unsafe, or destituting ourselves in order to fix it. Having to make that kind of choice is really hard.[11]*

The phrase "one paycheck away from poverty" is particularly apt in describing the situations for many of these households.

Other work has revealed parallel findings. Studies examining blue-collar or working-class families have found a similar dynamic.[12] As a result of less-marketable skills and education, these households experience a heightened vulnerability to economic deprivation and poverty. For example, the title of Lillian Rubin's book, *Families on the Faultline*, exemplifies this notion with regard to working class families. As Rubin wrote:

> *These are the men and women, by far the largest part of the American work force, who work at the lower levels of the manufacturing and service sectors of the economy; workers whose education is limited, whose mobility options are severely restricted, and who usually work for an hourly rather than a weekly wage. . . . They go to work every day to provide for their families, often at jobs they hate. But they live on the edge. Any unexpected event—a child's illness, an accident on the job, a brief layoff—threatens to throw them into the abyss.*[13]

Consequently, lower levels of marketable human capital put individuals at a greater risk of experiencing detrimental life course events that can create economic shocks. These, in turn, significantly increase the risk of poverty and economic turmoil for such households. I described this dynamic in earlier work as analogous to a set of dominoes. Once an unanticipated or detrimental event occurs, it can set in motion a domino effect that causes repercussions throughout an individual's daily life, with the end result being a spell in poverty.

INCREASING RISK AND VULNERABILITY IN AMERICAN SOCIETY

We can also consider economic vulnerability on a more macro level. Economic and societal changes have placed those with less human capital in an even more precarious position over time. During the past several decades, economic insecurity has been rising, particularly for those in the bottom half of income distribution.

The political scientist Jacob Hacker was one of the first to describe these changes as part of a "great risk shift."[14] From the mid-1970s onward, greater economic risk has been shifted from government and employers onto the backs of workers and their families. As a result, the life course risk of poverty has been on the rise.[15]

The declining percentage of good jobs that can adequately support a family is indicative of this change. When we speak of good jobs, one is generally referring to jobs that pay a livable wage, have benefits, are relatively stable, and possess good working conditions. They are the backbone of the American dream of economic security.[16] Yet, such jobs have been harder to come by in more recent times.

Volumes of research have been written about this and why it has occurred. A number of factors are suggested to account for the loss of such jobs, including globalization and outsourcing, increased international competition, technological change that benefits highly educated workers, corporate restructuring, the decline of unions and worker power, expansion of the service sector, and the weakening of government intervention in the labor market.[17]

The result has been a proliferation of lower quality jobs during the past few decades. This can be illustrated in several ways. First, it is estimated that approximately 40% of all jobs today are low paying, that is, jobs paying less than $16 an hour.[18] Indicative of this has been the fact that male median full-time wages between 1973 and 2021 have been stagnate in real dollar terms. In 1973, the median wage was $61,140 (in 2021 dollars), and by 2021 it was $61,180.[19] In other words, the typical male worker in the United States has seen a total wage gain of 40 dollars across these 49 years, or less than one dollar on an annual basis. Low-wage jobs also frequently lack benefits. In particular, decent and affordable healthcare, pensions, sick leave, vacation time, and other benefits are increasingly absent from low-wage work.[20]

Second, there has been a tendency for greater numbers of jobs being created to be part time rather than full time.[21] Many of these part-time jobs offer no benefits whatsoever. In an average month in 2021, there were approximately five million Americans working part time, because either their hours had been cut back or they were unable to find full-time work.[22]

Third, the numbers of unemployed and the length of time that individuals remain unemployed has been rising over the past five decades.

In the 1960s, the notion of "full employment" was considered an unemployment rate of 3% to 4%, whereas today, 5% to 6% is considered the norm, although unemployment has been quite variable over recent years. In addition, the percentage of workers out of a job for a prolonged period of time has been rising steadily over the past 50 years. Over the last few years, approximately 40% of the unemployed have been out of work for 27 weeks or more, which is an all-time high.[23] And as a result of the pandemic, many older workers have simply left the labor market.

Fourth, work in general has become much more unstable and precarious.[24] Individuals are at a greater risk today of being laid off or released from their job than in the past. This includes both low- and high-quality jobs.

Fifth, there have been limited sectors of the economy that have seen the creation of good-quality jobs over the last few decades. In particular, the financial and technology sectors of the labor market have produced a number of jobs with good wages and benefits.[25]

Finally, as a result of these trends, there appears to be an increasing level of polarization in the labor market.[26] A number of the new jobs that have been created are of low quality, while a smaller number of jobs are of fairly high quality. The gap between the haves and have nots has widened, while the middle ground has been hollowing out. Taken together, these changes in the labor market and economy suggest that the landscape of opportunity has become more tilted over time.

The result of all of this is that it has become harder for each generation to do better economically than the previous generation. The research of economist Raj Chetty and colleagues has shed light on this pattern.[27] Chetty has been at the forefront of using big data to analyze what has happened to economic mobility in the United States over time. In this analysis, he merged data from the Census Bureau with individual federal income tax returns. The result was a total of more than 10 million parent-child pairs within the analysis. Chetty and colleagues were looking at parents' household income between the ages of 25 and 35 years and comparing that with their child's household income at age 30 years.

In the top panel of Figure 4.1, we can see how well children who were born in 1940, 1950, 1960, 1970, and 1980 were doing in comparison with their parent's income. For children born in 1940, nearly all of them earned more than their parents earned. Obviously, for those whose parents were earning very little (i.e., the fifth percentile), there is little way but up for their children to go. However, regardless of how much their parents were earning, almost all children from the 1940 cohort were earning more as adults. Only for those children whose parents were at the very top end of the income distribution (i.e., the top 95th percentile) did the percentages begin to drop. Altogether, over 90% of children born in 1940 would go on to earn more than their parents earned.

However, what we can see is that for the 1950, 1960, 1970, and 1980 birth cohorts, there was a steady decline in the likelihood of children earning more than their parents. For each decade, the curve dropped lower, such that by 1980, only children whose parents were in the bottom 40% of the income distribution were able on average to earn more than their parents.

The bottom panel of Figure 4.1 shows this in a slightly different way. Here, we have the yearly birth cohorts from 1940 to 1984 and the overall average percentage of the entire cohort surpassing their parents' income. We see a dramatic decline over time in the likelihood of children earning more than their parents. As Chetty noted: "Absolute mobility declined starkly across birth cohorts: On average, 92% of children born in 1940 grew up to earn more than their parents. In contrast, only 50% of children born in 1984 grew up to earn more than their parents."[28]

Consequently, the overall patterns of absolute mobility in the United States showed a steady decline. Chetty wrote: "Children's prospects of earning more than their parents have faded over the past half-century in the United States. . . . Absolute income mobility has fallen across the entire income distribution, with the largest declines for families in the middle class."[29]

In illustrating the changes related to growing economic insecurity, many real-life examples could be given. For purposes of space, however, I focus on two individuals from my *Chasing the American Dream* book.

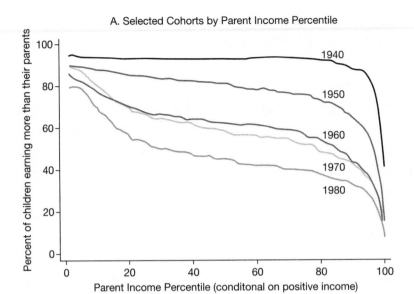

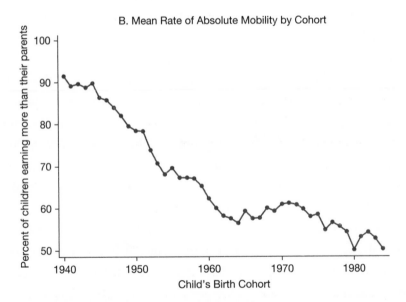

Figure 4.1 Absolute intergenerational mobility for birth cohorts from 1940 to 1980.
SOURCE: Raj Chetty, David Grusky, Maximilian Hell, Nathaniel Hendren, Robert Manduca, and Jimmy Narang, "The Fading American Dream: Trends in Absolute Income Mobility since 1940," NBER Working Paper Series, Working Paper 22910, National Bureau of Economic Research, Cambridge, MA, December 2016.

The first was employed at a big box retail store, while the second found himself in a declining industry.

In the 1950s and 1960s, General Motors was the largest private employer in the country. Today it is Walmart. When I met Edgar Williams, he had just arrived home from work, still wearing his dark blue janitor uniform. Edgar, who was 58 and African American, worked at Walmart for several years and was currently employed at Sam's Club (which is also owned and operated by Walmart). His working conditions epitomize the changes discussed at the lower wage levels. Sitting in his living room, Edgar talked about these conditions:

What they're trying to do now is kill all full-time work like Walmart did and make it part-time so they don't have to pay benefits. So that's their goal.

You don't know when they're going to let you go. Because they want to replace you with part-time people. They gonna hire two part timers for one full time. I only make $11.60 an hour, and I've been there all this time. Then they've got a ceiling where some of the people that have been there 20, 22 years, they've gone as far as they can go, they can't go no further in salary. They cap the salary.

They used to be a good company to work for. They used to give merit raises. Now, if you get a 60 cent raise a year, you're doing good. If they give you 40 cents, you're doing alright, and a lot people don't get none. And it's bad. It's bad. But the public don't know it [chuckle].

And this is the thing, the worst part, they make you have open availability. Where they can schedule you any kind of way, so that don't give you no room for another job. You know, because you don't have a set schedule.

Sometimes I get really, really irritated. And I don't curse or nothing, but I tell them how I feel. They get up in the morning and they do their little Sam's cheer. And one time they asked me, "How come you don't cheer?" I said, "I will when ya'll stop lying. When you said, members are number one, because that's not true."

You remember that commercial that used to come on years ago when the man got stuck in the revolving door [laughter]. That's the way you feel. You're just going around and around and around. It's cruel. It's cruel. We supposed to be the richest country in the world, and you want to help somebody, but in this country, you want to cut out everything for the lower income people.[30]

The working conditions that Edgar described at Sam's and Walmart are typical of the job conditions in much of the low-wage service sector of the economy. These are jobs that are extremely difficult to survive and support a family on.

For Greg Owens, his American dream was to land a job as a reporter with a major newspaper. He started his journalism career at several small papers, but eventually worked his way up to the city's long-established and well-respected newspaper, first as a part-timer and then full time. As Greg said: "Obviously I was excited when I got the job. It took almost a year, but I did, and I'm still there today."

Yet Greg has seen the dramatic cutbacks and volatility that has been occurring in the print media industry across the country in recent years. He discussed at length the insecurity facing his colleagues at the paper:

The dark periods were probably two or three years ago when they just started laying people off. And you're sitting there, and you see someone sitting in the chair one minute, they're called into an office, and then they're gone. After 30 years at this paper. And they don't have a chance to say goodbye. They don't have a chance to have a farewell party or anything.

Their choices are you can go back to your desk and gather your belongings while someone's standing over your shoulder. Or you can walk out, and we'll just pack it up and bring it to your house later. So you're stripped of . . . you know, for some people, this is their identity. Their chief identity is they're an editor. They're a reporter. They have some sort of status in the community, and now they're unemployed. So that was really hard to watch.

The point is that you're working in this environment where the sense of security is completely gone. It's sort of like a game of survivor. I mean you come in every day, and it's like who's going to be gone? And really, what are you winning at the end of the day? You're not winning a million dollars, you're just winning the right to a paycheck.

The newspaper had been sold a few years after Greg started his reporting, and the new owners were seeking concessions and salary cutbacks from the workers:

In the midst of all of this was a Union contract that had to be negotiated. And we all had to agree to a 6 percent pay cut, which actually ended up being almost 8 percent.

So in the midst of layoffs, and then to get your salary cut on top of that, I went into this like funk because now I'm in my mid 40's at the time. And you usually think you're sort of just in this trajectory. Slow but steady your income continues to rise, which it had, but now it's like, what's going to happen? I'm never going to be at that point again.

It does affect your morale. You sort of feel like, have I plateaued? Is this as good as it gets? I mean you want to keep working hard and making more money obviously. And I'm not in a position to do that. So then you sort of think about what does 8 percent of my life represent because it's 8 percent of my salary.

It's sort of a punch in the gut. Everybody at work is that way. It was kind of numb for a lot of people because we basically voted to cut ourselves, our pay. And it's sort of like cutting off your arm to like . . .

To save your body?

It's like that movie [127 Hours]. Okay, so I'm still alive, but I don't have an arm.[31]

These two examples illustrate the rising vulnerability that workers are facing as a result of the changing nature of jobs. As a result, more

Americans, particularly those with lower levels of human capital, are at risk. As Hacker has shown, downward swings in income volatility have become more pronounced over time.

Another major macro change that has hit those with less human capital particularly hard has been the attacks on the social safety net. Since the election of Ronald Reagan in 1980, the social protections and programs available to lower income households have seen retrenchment.[32] Programs such as TANF (Temporary Assistance for Needy Families), SNAP (Supplemental Nutrition Assistance Program), and Medicaid have been under attack, while the minimum wage has stagnated in terms of its purchasing power.[33] Other protections such as pension plans and union coverage have withered away.

An example of someone who encountered this heightened risk of poverty and economic turmoil over time was Julie Lopez, another individual interviewed in my *Chasing the American Dream* book. Julie and her husband, Victor, lived in a rural subdivision about 45 minutes outside the main metropolitan area. On the day we visited, the road leading into her neighborhood was riddled with large potholes, and there were several signs of foreclosure in front of houses on the street. Julie's house was quite small, and as we sat around the kitchen table, it quickly became apparent that the family was experiencing economic troubles.

Julie and her husband had both worked at a factory producing seats for minivans. Julie, who turned 40, had been employed at the plant for 17 years. Between her and her husband's incomes, they were able to maintain a solid middle-class lifestyle. However, as Julie explained, the company decided to close the factory and move it to Canada.

At first I think everybody was just stunned. They were like "Oh no."
Didn't want to believe it. And then the closer it got, it was like "Oh no!"
Then they had that panic and that fear. "What am I going to do? How
am I going to provide for my family? I need health insurance." Because
a lot of people needed that health insurance. 'Cause there was a big
diversity of people down there working. I mean from teenagers all the

way up to 60 some odd years old people. There was a lot of panic, and some of them people down there already went through a plant closure.

How did they tell you?

Oh! They just called a big town hall meeting out in the docks and said "We're closing the doors October 28th" or something like that.

Julie's husband had since gotten a job driving a truck that hauled fuel, but Julie remained unemployed. In addition, their daughter Gabby had a birth defect that has caused her to have multiple surgeries. They have struggled financially, experiencing poverty and debt. Julie talked about these changes:

We were so used to that lifestyle. So when I lost my job, there goes the newspaper, the magazines, our entertainment went down to nil, I mean absolutely nothing because we had to pay our bills first. So that was quite a struggle. I guess we've lived here for 16 years, and then things start falling apart after 16 years, and it's like "Ugh."

The security that they once felt they had was now gone:

I don't feel secure at all. I mean Victor and I no longer contribute to our 401s. They're just sitting there idle, and we're not getting any younger, which worries me. . . . I just don't have that security feel since I'm unemployed.

In addition, because of the drop in income there has been additional stress introduced into their family. It has become much harder to maintain some semblance of normality.

You know, Victor works 14 hours a day. He comes home, he's bone tired, does his work, and he goes to bed. And then on the weekends when he does have off, he's trying to make up that family time.[34]

Julie Lopez is but one of many examples that illustrate how the macro-economic changes that have been occurring over recent decades have increased the vulnerability of those with less human capital.

Being non-White further increases the economic vulnerability that individuals may face. Persons of color are much more likely to encounter discrimination in the labor market. An example of this is Denise Turner, who I interviewed in my *Living on the Edge* book.

> *This is an extremely racist city. And the racism is very subtle. It's very difficult for an intelligent black person to find anything of substance to do in this city. And that's one of my major problems that I'm encountering now.*
>
> *I have a job now which is paying minimum wage. Not using any of my skills. I'm working at a toy store. You know, I can do plenty of that. I can do plenty of waiting tables. And I can be at McDonald's and Burger King. But that is not what I want to do! And it's not gonna pay me to raise four children. To take anything that's gonna pay minimum wage, it's just not gonna work out. And I have discussed this with my case workers. And they say, "Hey, it's just not gonna pay you. It's not gonna work out for you." To get a job paying minimum wage is not gonna work out. And so getting a job is difficult. I don't even think there are any jobs here.*[35]

Even for those who obtain greater skills and education, they still may face the additional barrier of discrimination. In one of the focus groups for the *Chasing the American Dream* book, there was a heated and heart-felt discussion about the role that discrimination plays in holding African Americans and other persons of color back in the job market. John Hudson conveyed this story:

> *Let me tell you, a lot people say, "You know, African Americans, don't complain. Try hard and you'll get far. And put your head down, don't be lazy and do this." My brother works for the Long Island Railroad for 10 years. He went from a station cleaner to an electrician. You see you're*

dealing with people's emotions. This is in Long Island. A few white guys is prejudice. My brother was the only black guy with electricians on the railroad. About seven of them. He came to the locker and seen a guy putting on his locker, "Nigger we're gonna push you in front of a train." My brother was saying "What you doing?" He say "Nah I was just reading it." He said "You put that up there." The guy said, "No I didn't." They investigated. The tape that was on the locker, on the inside, they found the guy's fingerprint. That's why my brother sued the railroad for $85,000. And now he's not an electrician. He's a car inspector. They dropped him from an electrician back to a station cleaner because he made a fuss about it and he sued them.

So the point is my brother worked hard, he wanted to be an electrician. But because somebody was in a position, a supervisor, he discriminated against my brother. Maybe because my brother is a dark skin African American, and I'm light skinned. He didn't like him.

So my brother did right. He went to school. He went to electrician school. He worked in Babylon. He lived in the Bronx. He had to leave at 3 o'clock in the morning to get to Babylon at 6 because they were putting the pressure on him. In other words, "Quit if you don't like it." My brother said, "No, I'm gonna keep going to this electric class, 6 in the morning." He did, put his head down, was quiet, worked hard, and then look what happened. He seen a guy put that on [the sign on his locker], he sued the railroad, he got paid.

But I mean now look. How far do you think my brother is going to get on the railroad? The only thing he probably can be is an inspector right now. That's all, that's what he is. They dropped him down to a car station cleaner again. Now he's a car inspector. That's the most he can probably be because they're looking at him, "Yeah, you know who that is. He sued us, he got Ralph or Johnny fired."

John went on to say that even for African Americans who do make it, they still often face the burden of discrimination:

Some do slip through. But they pay that extra cost. Like the black doctor who drives his BMW and constantly gets pulled over by the cops in New York City. Or the black actress who gets a standing ovation on Broadway after a show, and she can't catch a cab in midtown. It's deep. It's, it's real deep.

You talk about black citizens, they are disproportionally the poorest citizens in America. And it's not a question of how or why. Blacks never got the same chance, the same fair start the rest of Americans have gotten. Not to mention, hundreds and hundreds of years of exposure to white supremacy, scientific racism, government policies that inspire racial self-hate. Black self doubt is still a growth industry in America.[36]

For African Americans and other persons of color, a series of subtle and not so subtle acts of discrimination in the job market serve to intensify the effect of cumulative disadvantage.[37] Such acts of discrimination have been demonstrated in a multitude of court cases and research studies.[38] One of the best known of the recent analyses was conducted by two economists, Marianne Bertrand and Sendhil Mullainathan.[39] The researchers sent out similar résumés to various job ads in Chicago and Boston. The one differ-ence was that some of the résumés had "White-sounding" names, while the others had "Black-sounding names." Even though the résumés were virtually identical, those with White-sounding name résumés were 50% more likely to be contacted by the employer than the Black-sounding name résumés. This and many other studies have clearly shown that dis-crimination on the basis of race and ethnicity is alive and well in the job market and consequently influences the life chances of individuals.

CONCLUDING NOTE

The first factor in understanding the occurrence of poverty is the concept of economic vulnerability and the role that the lack of human capital plays in accentuating such vulnerability. People who have fewer skills and edu-cation, or who possess other attributes putting them at a disadvantage in terms of competing in the labor market (e.g., single parenthood, having a disability, or being non-White), are more likely to experience detrimental economic events, while at the same time being more adversely affected when they occur. These episodes often result in pushing individuals and families below the poverty line.

This first component of the structural vulnerability model explains who is at greater risk of experiencing poverty through the lack of human capital. We now turn to the second element of the model, which addresses why such individuals are lacking human capital in the first place.

Cumulative Inequality

In the previous chapter, we examined the role that the lack of human capital plays in increasing an individual's economic vulnerability, particularly poverty. In this chapter, we ask, given that skills and education bear on the risk of poverty (by causing varying degrees of vulnerability), why are individuals lacking these in the first place? A major reason lies in the importance of cumulative inequality. This is the second component of the structural vulnerability framework.

Analyses of the American system of stratification have shown that while some amount of social mobility does occur, social class as a whole tends to reproduce itself.[1] Those with working or lower class parents are likely to remain working or lower class themselves.[2] Similarly, those whose parents are affluent are likely to remain affluent.[3] Why? The reason is that parental class differences result in significant differences in the resources and opportunities available to their children. These differences in turn affect children's future life chances and outcomes, including the accumulation of skills and education. This process of cumulative advantage or disadvantage results in widening inequalities over time.

While it is certainly possible for someone to rise from rags to riches, that tends to be much more the exception rather than the rule. Lillian Rubin explained:

Our denial notwithstanding, then, class inequalities not only exist in our society, they're handed down from parents to children in the same

way that wealth is passed along in the upper class. True, American
society has always had a less rigid and clearly defined class structure
than many other nations. Poor people climb up; wealthy ones fall.
These often well-publicized figures help to fuel the myth about equality
of opportunity. But they're not the norm. Nor is the perpetuation of our
class structure accidental. The economy, the polity, and the educational
system all play their part in ensuring the continuity and stability of our
social classes.[4]

The impact of differences in income and social class from one generation
to the next is therefore a critical factor in understanding the human capital and skill differences that exist in today's society.

A game analogy helps to illustrate this process. The quintessential
American board game is that of Monopoly. The objective of the game is to
acquire properties, build houses and hotels, collect rent, make money, and
eventually put the other players out of business. The rules themselves are
straightforward. Normally, each player is given $1,500 at the start of the
game. The playing field is in effect level, with each of the players' outcomes
determined by the roll of the dice and their own skills and judgments.

This notion of a level playing field is largely the way that we like to
imagine the economic race in America is run as discussed in Chapter 3.
Each individual's outcome is determined by their own skill and effort and
by taking advantage of what happens along the road of life. Our belief in
equality of opportunity as a nation underlies this principle.

However, let us now imagine a modified game of Monopoly, in which
the players start out with quite different advantages and disadvantages,
much as they do in life. Player 1 begins with $5,000 and several Monopoly
properties on which houses have already been built. Player 2 starts out
with the standard $1,500 and no properties. Finally, Player 3 begins the
game with only $250.

The question becomes who will be the winners and losers in this modified game of Monopoly? Both luck and skill are still involved, and the rules
of the game remain the same, but given the differing sets of resources and
assets that each player begins with, these become much less important in

predicting the game's outcome. Certainly, it is possible for Player 1, with $5,000 to lose, and for Player 3, with $250, to win, but that is unlikely given the unequal allocation of money at the start of the game. Moreover, while Player 3 may win in any individual game, over the course of hundreds of games, the odds are that Player 1 will win considerably more often, even if Player 3 is much luckier and more skilled.

In addition, the way each of the three individuals are able to play the game will vary considerably. Player 1 is able to take greater chances and risks. And if they make several tactical mistakes, these probably will not matter much in the larger scheme of things. If Player 3 makes one such mistake, it may very well result in disaster. Player 1 will also be able to purchase properties and houses that Player 3 is largely locked out of, causing the rich to get richer and the poor to get poorer. These assets, in turn, will generate further income later in the game for Player 1 and in all likelihood will result in the bankrupting of Players 2 and 3.

Consequently, the initial advantages or disadvantages at the start of the game result in additional advantages or disadvantages as the game progresses. These, in turn, will then lead to further advantages or disadvantages, and so the process goes.

This analogy illustrates the concept that Americans are not beginning their lives at the same starting point.[5] But it also illustrates the cumulative process that compounds advantages or disadvantages over time. Differences in parental incomes and resources exert a major influence over children's ability to acquire valuable skills and education. These differences in human capital will, in turn, strongly influence how well children compete in the labor market and therefore help to determine the extent of their economic success during the course of their lives, as well as their risk of poverty. In short, inequality of outcomes leads to inequality of opportunities.

In this chapter, we explore this second major component of the structural vulnerability perspective. The argument is that as a result of the position one starts in life, particular advantages or disadvantages may be present. These initial advantages or disadvantages can then result in further advantages or disadvantages, producing a cumulative process in which inequalities are widened across the life course. The failure or success in acquiring valuable human capital is often the result of this process.

One of the earliest discussions addressing this topic was an analysis of scientific productivity by the sociologist Robert Merton.[6] Merton argued that early recognition, placement, and advantage in the career of a young scientist often led to exponential gains and rewards over time, which in turn further solidified the status and reputation of the scientist. Scientists who did not experience these key early advantages (although they were quite as capable) generally saw their careers stall and plateau. Merton described cumulative advantage as "the way in which initial comparative advantage of trained capacity, structural location, and available resources make for successive increments of advantages such that the gaps between the haves and the have-nots . . . widen."[7] Merton referred to this process as the "Matthew effect." Since Merton's initial discussions, this concept has been applied in a wide array of subjects, including differences in schooling, work and career opportunities, and overall health status.[8]

Let us then explore in the pages ahead several of the more apparent ways in which cumulative inequality operates across the life course. Within these examples, I focus on two major fault lines in American society that are particularly poignant in illustrating cumulative advantage and disadvantage: class and race. These two factors exert a profound influence on people's life chances and their ability to acquire human capital.

THE PROCESS AND DYNAMICS
OF CUMULATIVE INEQUALITY

The Geography of Disadvantage

We begin our exploration of cumulative inequality with a look at the types of neighborhoods that children grow up in, specifically with respect to race and income. The neighborhood a child is raised in can have a profound impact on that child's future well-being and life chances, and the neighborhood one is brought up in is highly dependent on a child's class and race. Growing up in a high-poverty neighborhood can be particularly detrimental, whereas growing up in an affluent neighborhood generally carries significant advantages.

Over the past 30 years, researchers have focused on the economic well-being of the neighborhoods that individuals reside in as one way to describe and understand the nature of American poverty. The argument is that neighborhoods mired in poverty detrimentally affect all who reside in such communities and are particularly harmful to children. For example, Paul Jargowsky posed the question: "Why should we be concerned with the spatial organization of poverty?" His answer is the following:

> *The concentration of poor families and children in high-poverty ghettos, barrios, and slums magnifies the problems faced by the poor. Concentrations of poor people lead to a concentration of the social ills that cause or are caused by poverty. Poor children in these neighborhoods not only lack basic necessities in their own homes, but also they must contend with a hostile environment that holds many temptations and few positive role models. Equally important, school districts and attendance zones are generally organized geographically, so that the residential concentration of the poor frequently results in low-performing schools.*[9]

Research indicated that even after controlling for individual income and race, children's well-being in high-poverty neighborhoods suffers in many ways.[10] For example, Margery Turner and Deborah Kaye found that, independent of individual characteristics: "As a neighborhood's poverty rate rises, so too does the likelihood of negative behavior among young children, of being expelled from school, of negative school engagement, of lack of involvement in activities, of not being read to or taken on outings, of living in a family with no full-time workers, and of having a caretaker who is aggravated or in poor mental health."[11]

This neighborhood context of poverty has been particularly significant in the seminal work of William Julius Wilson,[12] Douglas Massey,[13] and Robert Sampson.[14] Their research has shown that children growing up in high-poverty neighborhoods suffer from many disadvantages as a result of geographical residence. In addition, the children impacted by these negative effects are often children of color due to the long-established patterns of residential racial segregation in American cities.

The opposite is true for children growing up in middle-class or affluent neighborhoods. Here we find an environment that is likely to facilitate individual growth and development. Such neighborhoods are characterized by good schools, low crime, plentiful recreational facilities, quality housing, and so on. The result is a strong foundation on which children are able to develop their potential.

In addition, research has indicated that there has been a rise in residential segregation on the basis of income over the last 30 years.[15] Douglas Massey discussed this growing trend in his often-quoted 1995 presidential address to the Population Association of America: "The Age of Extremes: Concentrated Affluence and Poverty in the Twenty-First Century."[16] Massey noted that the separation of the haves from the have-nots was becoming wider and would likely continue to do so into the future.

Growing up in high-poverty neighborhoods is therefore a significant disadvantage and represents a starting point for cumulative disadvantage, just as growing up in an affluent neighborhood is a significant advantage. In an analysis based on census tract data for 2000, Brett Drake and I focused on how many children in the United States were living in high-poverty neighborhoods. High-poverty neighborhoods were defined as census tracts in which 40% or more of children in the tract were in poverty. We constructed a second measure that looked at the likelihood of children residing in census tracts in which 40% or more of children from the same race/ethnicity fell into poverty. Our analysis was based on approximately 65,000 census tracts found in the United States. As discussed in Chapter 2, we can think of these tracts as roughly analogous to neighborhoods.

Table 5.1 shows the results from this analysis. The Columns 2 and 3 look at all children in the United States. We can see that while only 3.7% of White children were living in high-poverty neighborhoods, the percentage for Black children was 26.2% and for Hispanic children, 18.1%.

Table 5.1 PERCENTAGE OF CHILDREN BY RACE/ETHNICITY LIVING IN
HIGH-POVERTY NEIGHBORHOODS

Race/ethnicity	All Children		Poor Children	
	Across Race	Within Race	Across Race	Within Race
White	3.7%	3.0%	14.6%	13.7%
Black	26.2%	37.3%	43.5%	61.9%
Hispanic	18.1%	24.6%	33.1%	45.8%
All	8.7%	—	26.7%	—

SOURCE: U.S. Census Bureau, Drake and Rank calculations.

NOTE: High poverty neighborhoods defined as census tracts with 40% or greater
levels of poverty.

Using our second measure of neighborhood poverty shows even sharper
differences: 3.0% for White children, 37.3% for Black children, and 24.6%
for Hispanic children. Consequently, Black children were more than seven
times as likely as White children to be residing in high childhood poverty
neighborhoods, and they were over 12 times more likely to be residing
in a high childhood poverty neighborhood among children of the same
race. For Hispanic children, the divide between White children was nearly
as wide.

The Columns 4 and 5 in Table 5.1 examine the living arrangements of
children who themselves are poor. This illustrates to what extent children are at a double disadvantage when it comes to poverty; that is, not
only are they and their families living below the poverty line, but also the
neighborhoods they reside in are poverty stricken with respect to their
childhood peers as well. While 14.6% of poor White children were living
in high-poverty neighborhoods, 43.5% and 33.1% of poor Black and
Hispanic children, respectively, were residing in poverty neighborhoods.
Once again our second measure of neighborhood poverty is even more
extreme: 13.7% for poor White children, 61.9% for poor Black children,
and 45.8% for poor Hispanic children.

Consequently, Black and Hispanic children are routinely exposed to
high levels of neighborhood poverty when growing up compared to their
White counterparts. Exposure to such poverty can have a profound impact

on one's life chances, with the process of cumulative inequality starting at an early age.

As troubling as these findings are with respect to the racial/ethnic divide in neighborhood poverty, what is just as troubling is evidence indicating that mobility out of such neighborhoods is often difficult. Lincoln Quillian has shown that for Black residents living in high-poverty census tracts (40% or more poverty), nearly 50% were still residing in a high-poverty census tract 10 years later.[17] Even more disturbing, sociologist Patrick Sharkey found that 72% of Black children growing up in the poorest quarter of American neighborhoods remained in the poorest quarter of neighborhoods as adults. Consequently, the effects of neighborhood poverty on children of color are typically prolonged and long lasting.[18]

Furthermore, because Black homeowners are likely to buy homes later than Whites, and to purchase homes in lower income neighborhoods, the amount of equity that they have built up is substantially less than in the White population.[19] The result is that in 2018 overall median net worth for Whites was $166,000, whereas for Blacks it was $8,178.[20] This 20-to-1 difference in wealth then has a further cumulative effect on the life chances and well-being of children.

The work of economist Raj Chetty and colleagues has also demonstrated the profound effect of the neighborhood one is raised in on future life chances.[21] Chetty et al. showed that there are wide differences in upward mobility depending on childhood neighborhood. Children growing up in disadvantaged neighborhoods are much less likely to experience economic upward mobility than children growing up in economically thriving neighborhoods, even after taking into account individual socioeconomic and demographic differences.

In addition, children raised in neighborhoods marked by high poverty are much more likely to encounter a variety of environmental health hazards. These include elevated exposure to various toxic pollutants, greater likelihood of being victimized by crime and violence, higher arrest rates, increased risk of substance abuse, greater exposure to sexually transmitted diseases, and so on.[22] All of these can detrimentally affect a child's health, which in turn can have a profound impact on that child's health and economic well-being as an adult.[23]

Similarly, as I discuss in the next section, children living in high-poverty neighborhoods are quite likely to be attending educationally inferior neighborhood schools. Financing for public schools in the United States is largely drawn from local property tax revenues, resulting in poorer districts having a much smaller tax base to draw on than wealthier districts. As Steven Durlauf noted: "Despite the existence of state and federal programs to assist less affluent school districts, the role of local public finance in education produces large disparities in educational expenditure across school districts."[24] The result is that schools in low income neighborhoods often find that their "teachers are frequently underpaid and over stressed, the physical facilities may be severely deteriorated and outdated, class sizes are often quite large, as well as many other disadvantages."[25] Such schools have been shown to produce lower levels of academic achievement among children than if those same children were attending schools with less poverty and more educational resources.[26] In addition, research has shown that the socioeconomic status of one's classmates has an important influence on a child's educational achievement, independent of that child's individual economic background.[27]

Finally, as noted previously, substantial ethnographic and empirical research has indicated that friends and peers who are impoverished can exert a negative influence on fostering a range of counterproductive attitudes and behaviors among children and adolescents. These include lower academic aspirations and achievement, greater likelihood of teenage pregnancy, increased chances of engaging in illegal activities, and so on.[28] The result of all this is that such children carry with them a significant disadvantage as they move through the educational system and into the labor market.

Schools and Education

Travel to any U.S. city and you are likely to observe a similar pattern over and over again. Begin your trip with a drive out to an affluent suburb. The schools you encounter there are likely to be impressive with respect to their physical facilities, the quality of their instruction, and the depth of their curriculum. Next, turn the car around and drive into a poor neighborhood, perhaps in the central city, and there you are likely to see quite the opposite: decaying schools, demoralized faculty, and districts facing a loss of accreditation. Finally, take a much further drive out into the remote countryside, and you may discover a school district with the fewest resources of all.

Right outside the door of my home such patterns can be easily found. Within a 10-minute drive is a highly regarded public high school in an affluent school district. In that district, the average amount of money spent per pupil is around $16,000. The education that students receive is among the best in the nation's public schools. Drive a few minutes further, and you may notice a private high school that could very well be mistaken for a small university campus. There the spending per pupil averages $30,000. The quality and options of courses offered to students are almost unlimited. Finally, travel 20 minutes in the opposite direction and you will reach a high school that is literally falling apart, where the average money spent per pupil is around $9,000. The school district has lost its accreditation, and its students are nearly all poor and children of color.

In each of these different schools we find American children, all in the same metropolitan area, yet it is clear that some are entitled to a first-rate education, while others are not. To say that these children are experiencing equality of opportunity or a level playing field is simply absurd. Rather, cumulative inequality is clearly operating within the system of education that we have in the United States. Where one lives and the size of one's parent's pocketbook largely determine the quality of education that children will receive. Over three decades ago, Jonathan Kozal referred to this situation as the "savage inequalities" of America.[29]

Unfortunately, it is as true today, if not more so, than it was 30 years ago. A report by the Department of Education began with the following statement: "While some young Americans—most of them white and affluent—are getting a truly world-class education, those who attend school in high poverty neighborhoods are getting an education that more closely approximates schools in developing countries."[30]

One reason for this is the way that public education is funded in this county. The United States is one of the very few industrialized countries where the bulk of funding for public schools comes from local and state tax dollars rather than from the federal government. In particular, the overall value of real estate in a school district is the key determinant of the amount of resources that district will have available. Consequently, children living in lower income neighborhoods tend to be enrolled in schools with far fewer resources and a lower quality of instruction than children living in well-to-do neighborhoods.[31]

In their book *The American Dream and the Public Schools*, Jennifer Hochschild and Nathan Scovronick noted:

> *School district boundaries help to provide such an advantage when they follow neighborhood lines that separate wealthy children from those who are poor and often nonwhite; school financing schemes have this effect when they are based on local property value and thereby create or maintain a privileged competitive position for wealthier children at the expense of the others. Tracking provides advantages when the best teachers or the most resources are devoted to a high track disproportionately filled with wealthier students.*[32]

Research also indicated that since the mid-1970s, schools have actually become more segregated on the basis of race and income. As Erica Frankenberg and colleagues observed, "Segregation for black students is rising in all parts of the U.S. Black students, who account for 15% of enrollment, as they did in 1970, are in schools that average 47% black students."[33] Furthermore, Latino students are even more segregated. The authors found that "the segregation of Latino students is now the most severe of any group and typically involves a very high concentration of poverty."[34]

Schools that are predominantly minority are also highly skewed in the direction of poverty and low income. Rather than reducing the differences and disadvantages that some children face, the structure of schooling in the United States further increases and exacerbates those differences.[35] As Hochschild and Scovronick stated:

Public schools are essential to make the American dream work, but schools are also the arena in which many Americans first fail. Failure there almost certainly guarantees failure from then on. In the dream, failure results from lack of individual merit and effort; in reality, failure in school too closely tracks structures of racial and class inequality. Schools too often reinforce rather than contend against the intergenerational paradox at the heart of the American dream.[36]

The intergenerational paradox that the authors referred to is that: "Inequalities in family wealth are a major cause of inequality in schooling, and inequalities of schooling do much to reinforce inequalities of wealth among families in the next generation—that is the intergenerational paradox."[37] Indeed, research has shown that the amount of education and wealth of parents is highly correlated with the educational levels achieved by their children.[38]

The cumulative advantages and disadvantages at the K through 12 level become further extended into the likelihood of graduating from high school and then completing a college degree.[39] Children from wealthier families are often able to attend top-flight private universities, children from middle-class backgrounds frequently enroll at public universities, while children from lower class backgrounds will probably not continue on to college at all, or if they do, are likely to attend a community or 2-year college. As Daniel McMurrer and Isabel Sawhill noted: "Family background has a significant and increasing effect on who goes to college, where, and for how long. With the reward for going to college greater than ever, and family background now a stronger influence over who reaps those rewards, the United States is at risk of becoming more class strati-fied in coming decades."[40]

In summarizing the research on education, neighborhood, and income, Greg Duncan and Richard Marmame wrote: "As the incomes of affluent and poor American families have diverged over the past three decades, so too has the educational performance of the children in these families. Test score differences between rich and poor children are much larger now than thirty years ago, as are differences in rates of college attendance and college graduation."[41] Unfortunately, it appears that we may be moving even further afield of a level playing surface when it comes to education.

Jobs and Earnings

The process of cumulative advantage and disadvantage continues after one's formal education is completed. The amount and quality of education that an individual receives are key determinants in locating and attaining a well-paying job and profession, or conversely, working at a dead-end, low-paying job or no job at all. Sociologist Arne Kalleberg wrote: "Although educational attainment cannot guarantee a good job, higher levels of edu-cation make acquiring a better job more likely, and the lack of education is certainly a major disadvantage in the new labor market."[42]

The quality and type of job that one works at is highly dependent on the quantity and quality of one's education. Those who fail to graduate from high school are often locked into a series of dead-end, less stable jobs throughout their working career.[43] On the other hand, those with a college or advanced degree are much more likely to find themselves in a well-paying and rewarding professional career that includes various benefits. Consequently, the cumulative advantages and disadvantages that begin with childhood and neighborhood continue through adolescence and early adulthood with educational differences and are then further ex-tended into the prime working years through occupational sorting.

Kalleberg argued that these educational and skill differences have be-come even more important in today's economy. As he wrote:

Differences in education and skill levels increasingly separate those workers who have good jobs from those who have bad jobs. . . . While more-educated and higher-skilled workers may not necessarily have more job security with a particular employer, their more marketable skills enhance their labor market security, which, in turn, generally provides them with higher earnings, greater control over their jobs, higher intrinsic rewards, and better-quality jobs overall.[44]

For African Americans and other non-Whites, a series of subtle and not so subtle acts of discrimination in the job market serve to intensify the effect of cumulative disadvantage. Such acts of discrimination have been demonstrated in a multitude of court cases and a range of research studies.[45]

In order to visually observe this effect, my colleague Tom Hirschl and I conducted an analysis in which we looked at the likelihood of experiencing poverty versus affluence across adulthood for Whites and Blacks.[46] Poverty was defined as falling below the official poverty line, and affluence was measured as households earning 10 or more times the poverty level. Our analysis was based on longitudinal data extracted from the Panel Study of Income Dynamics (PSID; discussed in greater detail in the next chapter).

Figure 5.1 compares the ratio of the cumulative percentage of poverty versus affluence for the White and Black populations as they move across the life course. In other words, for each population, what is the likelihood of achieving affluence versus poverty at various points during adulthood? Thus, at each of the 51 years contained in Figure 5.1, the cumulative history of poverty and affluence for both Whites and Blacks is being compared and plotted as a ratio of one to the other. Figure 5.1 therefore provides a cumulative road map into the chances of having experienced poverty versus affluence for the White and Black populations.

The one-to-one ratio line in the figure represents an identical likelihood of having encountered affluence versus poverty. Below the one-to-one line shows the extent to which the chances are greater that Americans have encountered poverty versus affluence, while the area above the one-to-one

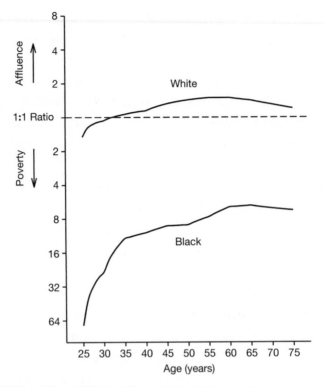

Figure 5.1 Affluence and poverty ratios for Whites and Blacks across adulthood.
SOURCE: Panel Study of Income Dynamics, Rank and Hirschl calculations.

line shows the extent to which the chances are greater that Americans
have encountered affluence versus poverty. Two sets of 51 cumulative
ratios (ages 25 to 75) for Whites and Blacks have been plotted in Figure
5.1. In order to show the full set of data within the figure, the cumulative
ratio scale along the *y* axis is logarithmic.

Figure 5.1 graphically portrays the racial differences in the likelihood of
encountering poverty versus affluence across the life course. We can see
that for Whites during their early adulthood years, the odds are somewhat
higher that they have experienced poverty versus affluence. This, of course,
makes sense in that younger adults in their 20s and early 30s as a whole
are more likely to be poor and much less likely to be affluent. However,
by the age of 33, Whites cross the one-to-one line, and as a group become more likely to have experienced affluence rather than poverty. This

peaks during the prime earning years of the 50s, where the ratio is approximately 1.5 to 1, or 50% higher of having achieved affluence versus poverty. This then slowly declines, such that by age 75, the cumulative ratio at the end of adulthood of having achieved affluence versus poverty is 1.2 to 1. For Whites, therefore, America represents a society where from the early 30s onward there is a somewhat better probability of having achieved affluence in one's past than having suffered from poverty. The image of America as a land of opportunity and prosperity would appear to be reasonably viable among the White population as a whole.

For Black Americans, we see a radically different story. Throughout adulthood, Blacks are many times more likely to have experienced poverty than affluence. The ratio of poverty to affluence begins at 70 to 1 at age 25 and rises no higher than 6 to 1 during the early 60s. By the time Blacks reach the age of 75, the cumulative ratio stands at 6.7 to 1 of having experienced poverty rather than affluence during their adulthood. Consequently, for Black Americans, the United States reflects a society where the odds are overwhelming across the life course of experiencing poverty rather than affluence. The American dream of achieving economic prosperity and avoiding impoverishment is simply that—a dream.

Figure 5.2 presents a second way of categorizing the lifetime risk of experiencing poverty versus affluence. The American population is divided into three broad groupings: (1) individuals who will experience affluence but will never face poverty during their adult lifetime; (2) individuals who will experience poverty but will never encounter affluence during their lifetime; and (3) individuals who will experience neither affluence nor poverty or who will experience both affluence and poverty at some point during their adult lifetime. This represents a stratification typology based on an individual's ability to attain affluence and/or avoid poverty during their lifetime. These estimates were derived by building a series of life tables for poverty, affluence, and the likelihood of experiencing either, again using data from the PSID.

Figure 5.2 illustrates the sharp racial divide with respect to the likelihood of encountering these economic extremes across a lifetime. For White Americans, one-third of the population can look forward to

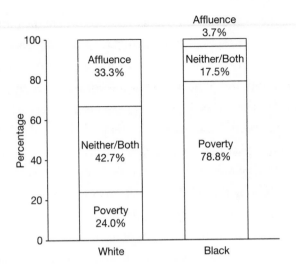

Figure 5.2 Economic extremes experienced by Whites and Blacks across adulthood from age 25 to 75.
SOURCE: Panel Study of Income Dynamics, Rank and Hirschl calculations.

encountering at least 1 year of economic affluence (and for many, they will enjoy economic prosperity over several years), with no risk of poverty during adulthood. On the other hand, approximately one-quarter of the White population will face at least 1 year below the poverty line (and again, these individuals are likely to encounter several spells of poverty across their adulthood years), with no prospect of ever attaining affluence during their lives. Finally, 42.7% of Whites lie between these top and bottom groups (21.2% will encounter neither poverty nor affluence, and 21.5% will encounter both).

For Black Americans, we see a sharp contrast in their lifetime chances of encountering affluence versus poverty. Only 3.7% of Blacks will encounter a year of affluence with no risk of poverty during their adulthood. On the other hand, nearly 80% of Black Americans will encounter poverty in their lives, with no chance of ever achieving affluence. Finally, 17.5% of Blacks fall between these two extremes (8.1% will encounter neither poverty nor affluence, while 9.4% will encounter both).

Taken together, Figures 5.1 and 5.2 reveal the vast racial economic divide in terms of encountering affluence versus being able to avoid poverty.

For White Americans, the chances are moderately better of encountering affluence rather than poverty during adulthood, but the risk of poverty is also quite real. For Black Americans, the chances of encountering poverty are enormous, while the odds of experiencing affluence are slim. Consequently, America would appear to represent a society where affluence and poverty are very real possibilities for Whites, whereas for Blacks, the American experience is captured by a staggering likelihood of encountering poverty during adulthood with little chance of attaining significant economic prosperity.

Health Disparities

A further cumulative advantage and disadvantage is the combined effect that educational background and socioeconomic status have on overall health and well-being. Beginning with the groundbreaking results from the Whitehall studies in England during the 1960s and 1970s, one of the most consistent findings in epidemiology has been the strong relationship between health and socioeconomic status. The lower the socioeconomic status (and particularly poverty), the more significant are the detrimental effects on health.[47] Poverty is associated with a host of health risks, including elevated rates of heart disease, diabetes, hypertension, cancer, infant mortality, mental illness, undernutrition, lead poisoning, asthma, dental problems, and a variety of other ailments and diseases.[48]

Conversely, the higher the socioeconomic status, the greater the positive impact on health. This relationship has been replicated in hundreds of studies over the years.[49] In addition, race has been found to have an additional independent effect on health status. African Americans, Hispanics, and Native Americans are more likely to suffer from various health problems, even after taking into account socioeconomic status, than are Whites.[50]

The process begins early. Research has demonstrated that the physical and mental well-being of children is strongly affected by socioeconomic status.[51] Perhaps most insidious is that children in lower income households are much more likely to be exposed to lead poisoning.[52] Children living in lower socioeconomic status households are also more likely to experience a range of health problems than children in higher socioeconomic status households. According to economist Bradley Schiller:

> *A child born to a poverty-stricken mother is likely to be undernourished both before and after birth. Furthermore, the child is less likely to receive proper postnatal care, to be immunized against disease, or even to have his or her eyes and teeth examined. As a result, the child is likely to grow up prone to illness and poverty, and in the most insidious of cases, be impaired by organic brain damage.*[53]

Poverty and low income are further associated with a host of health risks across the adulthood years, from elevated rates of heart disease to various chronic illnesses.[54] The result is a death rate for the poverty stricken approximately three times higher than that for the affluent between the ages of 25 and 64.[55] A very comprehensive study found that the life expectancy difference between adults with a master's degree versus those less than 12 years of education was approximately 14.7 years, while those in poverty had a life expectancy 10.5 years less than those with incomes over 400% of the poverty threshold.[56] Moreover, in many metropolitan areas, differences in residency based on zip code may produce a difference in life expectancy of up to 20 years.[57]

Older Adults

As a result of the dynamics of cumulative inequality across the life course, by the time individuals have reached retirement, these differences are often magnified, leaving many groups in dire financial and emotional straits.[58] Take the case of retirement savings. The amount one is able to accrue in a retirement account is largely dependent on the type of occupation that one has been employed in across a career. Individuals in good-paying jobs with generous benefits are often able to build a 401K account with a matching dollar amount from their employer. In other cases (although this has been in sharp decline), such individuals might be able to work toward a pension, resulting in a guaranteed monthly income during their retirement.

In addition, the amount that one eventually receives from Social Security is largely dependent on the amount contributed across the working years. Individuals in higher-paying jobs will have had greater deductions and therefore will receive more in Social Security when they retire.

On the other hand, those with fewer years of education and skills will generally find themselves in lower-paying jobs across the working years. As a result, they are less likely to have an adequate retirement savings plan or pension and have undoubtedly contributed much less into Social Security than their more fortunate counterparts. The result is that for a sizable percentage of the population, very little in assets and savings is waiting for them when they reach retirement; it is estimated that 21% of the retired population in 2018 had retirement savings of under $5,000.[59]

In this fashion, the process of cumulative inequality plays out in the final years. A history of cumulative advantage or disadvantage affects the extent to which individuals will be able to enjoy the later stages of life. Cumulative disadvantage produces a final indignity in the lives of those who must face its full impact.

OVERALL IMPACT

The assertion that the economic race is run as an altered game of Monopoly has been shown in the array of empirical work that we have been examining. From childhood through older age, prior advantages or disadvantages tend to multiply on each other.

However, we can also look at this process in terms of an overall effect. There are several ways we can measure and examine such an effect. These include the impact of a parent's income, occupation, and wealth on their adult offspring.

In one important study, analyses showed that if a father has a level of income that falls in the bottom 20% of the income distribution, 42.2% of the sons from such a father will wind up in the bottom quintile of the income distribution when they grow up, while only 7.9% will reach the top quintile in terms of the income distribution. On the other hand, if a father has an income in the top 20% of the income distribution, 36% of his sons will be earning an income in the top quintile of the income distribution, while only 9.5% will fall into the bottom quintile.[60]

Another way of conceptualizing this association is that research over the past 25 years has revealed a sizable correlation between father's and son's incomes, averaging around .5, indicated by what is known as an intergenerational elasticity statistic.[61] A correlation of .5 is approximately the correlation between fathers' and sons' heights. Thus, "if people's incomes were represented by their heights, the similarity in income between generations would resemble the similarity observed in the heights of fathers and sons."[62] More recent studies have found even higher correlations. For example, using Social Security records and longitudinal data for fathers' and sons' earnings, Bhashkar Mazumder reported an intergenerational correlation between .6 and .7.[63] This results in an even greater narrowing within our visual image of fathers' and sons' heights.

Research focusing on the transmission of occupational status has also found a strong connection between parents and children.[64] For example, Daniel McMurrer and Isabel Sawhill reported that children of professionals are "significantly more likely to become professionals as adults, and children of blue collar workers significantly more likely to work in blue collar occupations. . . . Men with white collar origins are almost twice as likely as those with blue collar origins to end up in upper white collar jobs."[65]

Or if one looks at the transmission of wealth, a similar pattern emerges.[66] William Gale and John Scholz estimated that intended family transfers and bequests account for 51% of current U.S. wealth, while an additional 12% is acquired through the payment of college expenses by parents. Consequently, nearly two-thirds of the net worth that individuals have acquired is through family transfers.[67] Parents with considerable wealth are able to pass on these assets and advantages to their children. As a result, it is estimated that "children of the very rich have roughly 40 times better odds of being very rich than do the children of the poor."[68]

Additional work has focused on the impact that growing up in poverty has on one's later economic well-being.[69] In our Monopoly example, this might represent the player beginning the game with $250. Joan Rodgers has found that of those who experienced poverty as an adult, 50% had experienced poverty as a child, while an additional 38% had grown up in homes that were defined as near poor (below 2.00 of the poverty line).[70] Once again, we see that the social class a child is reared in has a profound impact on their later economic well-being and outcomes.

This is not to say that economic movement is nonexistent. Individuals do move up and down the economic ladder across adulthood.[71] However, when such movement does happen, it often transpires over relatively short distances from their economic origins. In fact, contrary to popular myth, the United States tends to have less intergenerational mobility than a number of other industrialized countries,[72] and such mobility has been declining over time.[73] The empirical evidence clearly points to the fact that children from a lower class background will be much more at risk of economic vulnerability in their adult lives than children from wealthier families.

As I have argued throughout this chapter, the reasons for this are that children from a working or lower class background simply do not have the range and depth of opportunities as children from a middle- or upper-class background. This then affects the quantity and quality of human capital they are able to acquire. Likewise, the vast differences in educational quality by residence and income quickly illuminate the magnitude of these opportunity differences.[74]

Consequently, where one begins one's life exerts a powerful effect throughout the life course. This process was succinctly described by Howard Wachtel:

If you are black, female, have parents with low socioeconomic status, and [are] dependent upon labor income, there is a high probability that you will have relatively low levels of human capital which will slot you into low-paying jobs, in low wage industries, in low wage markets. With this initial placement, the individual is placed in a high risk category, destined to end up poor sometime during her working and nonworking years. She may earn her poverty by working fulltime. Or she may suffer either sporadic or long periods of unemployment. Or she may become disabled, thereby reducing her earning power even further. Or when she retires, social security payments will place her in poverty even if she escaped this fate throughout her working years. With little savings, wealth, or private pension income, the retiree will be poor.[75]

Thus, in order to understand why people are lacking in skills and education in the first place, one important place to look is the impact that a child growing up in a lower income and/or non-White family versus a child growing up in a well-to-do and/or White family has on that child's acquisition of human capital, which then impacts their economic outcomes. This process of cumulative inequality is often neglected in political and policy discussions, but unfortunately the class and race you are born into has wide-ranging implications on your life course. As Billie Holiday sang 80 years ago: "Them that's got shall get, them that's not shall lose. So the Bible says, and it still is news."

Two Levels of Understanding

A third key element of the structural vulnerability perspective is that there are two levels of understanding impoverishment. On one hand, we can ascertain who is more likely to experience poverty through the impact that human capital exerts on creating individual economic vulnerability, which was discussed in Chapter 4. On the other hand, why poverty occurs in the first place can be largely understood through various structural failings, which I discuss in this chapter. To illustrate these two levels, another analogy is used: that of musical chairs. The key is whether one chooses to analyze the losers of the game or the game itself.

MUSICAL CHAIRS

Let us imagine a game of musical chairs with 10 players but only 8 chairs. The players begin to circle around the chairs until the music stops. Who fails to find a chair? If we focus on the winners and losers of the game, some combination of luck and skill will be involved. In all likelihood, the losers will be those in an unfavorable position when the music stops, somewhat slower, less agile, and so on. In one sense, these are appropriately cited as the reasons for losing the game.

However, if we focus on the game itself, then it is quite clear that given only eight chairs, two players are bound to lose. Even if every player were suddenly to double his or her speed and agility, there would still be two losers. From this broader context, it really does not matter what the loser's characteristics are, given that two are destined to lose.

I would argue that this musical chairs analogy can be applied to America economically, socially, and politically. Given that there is unemployment, which translates into a shortage of jobs; given that we are producing more and more low-paying jobs that lack benefits; given that countless inner-city and rural communities have been devastated by economic restructuring; given the weak safety net in place to provide economic protection to the vulnerable; given that there is a scarcity of decent quality, affordable child care; given that there are few provisions to care for those who can no longer participate in the economy because of an illness—someone is going to lose at this game.

The losers will generally be those who have fewer skills, less education, and less training and therefore cannot compete as effectively and are more vulnerable than their counterparts who have acquired more skills and education. In one sense, we can focus on these deficits, such as a lack of education, as the reasons why individuals are at greater risk of becoming poor.

Yet if we focus on the game itself, then the causes of poverty move from the individual's lack of skills or education to the fact that the economy produces unemployment, creates low-paying jobs, bypasses low-income communities, offers few social supports and little protection, lacks affordable child care, or does not provide for those who can no longer participate economically due to an illness. These then become the more fundamental reasons for why people are poor in this country.

Certainly the degree and intensity of these structural failings may vary over time. In our musical chairs analogy, there may be 9 chairs for every 10 players or only 6 or 7. Likewise, the circumstances surrounding the economic game can and do change, which in turn affects the overall number of losers. Such changes result from a variety of factors, including economic upturns and downturns, public policy initiatives and changes, and demographic shifts in the population. The numbers of losers produced by the economic, social, and political systems in this country are therefore not written in stone.

For example, during the 1930s, the Great Depression resulted in a dramatic reduction in the number of economic opportunities, creating widespread unemployment and poverty.[1] During this period of time, the number of available chairs versus participants in the game was sharply reduced. More recently, the coronavirus pandemic resulted in a severe economic downturn, causing millions to face unemployment.[2] On the other hand, the 1960s saw a booming economy coupled with federal initiatives to address poverty. The result was a dramatic increase in the number of chairs available, resulting in a significant drop in the overall rates of poverty during the decade.[3]

Nevertheless, while the ratio of opportunities to participants fluctuates over time, at any given point there tends to be a significant number of losers produced by the overall game. What this means is that when we focus solely on personal characteristics, such as education, we can shuffle individual people up or down in terms of their being more likely to find a job, but we are still going to have somebody lose out if there are not enough decent-paying jobs to go around.

A similar analogy would be that greater education and more skills allow an individual to move further up in the overall queue of people looking to find a good-paying and rewarding job. However, because of the limited number of such jobs, only a set amount of people in the queue will be able to land such jobs. Consequently, one's position in the queue can change as a result of human capital, but the same amount of people will still be stuck at the end of the line if the overall opportunities remain the same. In short, we are playing a game of musical chairs in this country with 10 players but only 8 chairs.

EVIDENCE FOR THE LACK OF CHAIRS

Many examples and circumstances exist demonstrating the structural mismatch that exists in today's society. In this section, I review several of the more obvious ones. In each case, it is clear that there are many more players than there are chairs available.

Shortage of Livable Wage Jobs

Perhaps the most important evidence for failings at the structural level resulting in a lack of opportunities for all in need is the previously mentioned imbalance between the number of jobs that can support a family in the current economy and the number of families in need of such jobs. In his study of long-term unemployment, Thomas Cottle talked with one man who had worked for 25 years with the same company, only to have his job downsized. After 2½ years of searching, he eventually found a job at a much lower pay scale, but felt fortunate to have such a job nonetheless. He referred to his job search using the musical chairs analogy discussed previously:

> *The musical chairs of work still have me in the game. The music plays, we run around, the music stops and I dive for a chair. Took me two and half years to find this last one, I don't want the music to stop again. I'm only fifty-two, but pretty soon they'll take all the chairs away. Then what? That's the part I don't want to think about.*[4]

Or as one of the interviewees in my *Chasing the American Dream* book put it, there's a number of Americans who are thinking "the music's going to stop and they're not going to have a chair. And they're just probably living on the brink. One paycheck away, one car accident away, one unfortunate illness away" from joining those in poverty.[5]

As discussed in Chapter 4, over the past 50 years, the U.S. economy has been producing more and more low-paying jobs, part-time jobs, and jobs lack benefits. It is estimated that approximately 40% of all jobs in the United States for 2018 were low paying, that is, paying less than $16 an hour.[6] In addition, many of these jobs lack basic benefits, such as healthcare coverage, 401K plans or pensions, child care assistance, and so on.[7]

And of course, beyond these low-paying jobs, there are millions of Americans who are unemployed at any point in time. For example, during the past 40 years, U.S. monthly unemployment rates have averaged between 4% and 10%.[8] These percentages represent individuals who are out of work but are actively looking for employment. They do not include discouraged workers who have given up looking for work or individuals who are working part-time but want to be working full-time. Including these categories of workers results in an underemployment rate that is typically twice as high as the unemployment rate.

During 2021, the overall average monthly rate of unemployment was 5.3%, representing 8.6 million workers. Furthermore, the average number of individuals working part-time but wanting to work full-time was 4.9 million. In addition, the number of individuals not currently in the labor force but wanting a job was 6.3 million. If we combine these numbers, we arrive at an annual estimate of either unemployment or underemployment of approximately 12.2%.[9]

Moreover, it is important to note that the unemployment rate represents how many individuals are unemployed in a given month in time. If instead we focus on the likelihood of experiencing a spell of unemployment at some point across the entire period of 1 year, the numbers and percentages are much higher. For example, in 2017 the average number of Americans unemployed in any given month was approximately 7 million, representing an average unemployment rate of 4.4%. However, 15.6 million Americans experienced unemployment at some point during 2017, which translated into an annual unemployment rate of 8.6%.[10]

Table 6.1 contains an analysis that my colleague Steve Fazzari and I conducted using the March Current Population Survey. As mentioned in Chapter 4, this is the same survey used to derive the annual estimates of poverty and income. In this analysis, we sought to determine how many adequately paying jobs were available for the pool of labor looking for such a job. We included everyone currently employed, as well as the unemployed, along with those who wanted a job but were not technically in the labor force. We excluded individuals who were working part-time by choice. In addition, we confined the analysis to those between the ages of 25 and 59, which is often considered the prime working years. An adequately paying job was defined as one that paid more than twice the poverty line for a household of two. In 2020 that came out to a weekly wage of $663, or approximately $16.50 an hour.

Table 6.1 PERCENTAGE OF INDIVIDUALS IN THE LABOR FORCE AGE 25–59
WITHOUT AN ADEQUATELY PAYING JOB

Year	Percentage Not Holding an Adequately Paying Job
2020	30.7%
2015	36.7%
2010	39.0%
2005	35.0%
2000	33.4%

SOURCE: Current Population Survey, Fazzari and Rank calculations.

NOTE: Adequately paying job is defined as one paying twice the poverty line for a household of 2.

The first row indicates that in 2020, 30.7% of individuals were not working at a decent-paying job. For 2015, the figure was 36.7%; 39.0% for 2010; 35.0% for 2005; and 33.4% for 2000. Consequently, over the last 20 years approximately one out of three Americans working or wanting work were unable to secure an adequately paying job.

The result is that many individuals are left out in the cold when it comes to finding a livable wage job with benefits.[11] Such chairs have become hard to locate. On the other hand, a few of the remaining chairs have become more comfortable and spacious. That is, some of the jobs being created in the new economy pay very good wages with solid benefits. Many of these are found in the financial and technology sectors, as well as in several of the professional fields. The result has been that the gap between the bottom and top of society has been getting wider, with those in the top 20% of the income distribution the beneficiaries of virtually all of the economic gains over the past 50 years.

Geographical Spatial Mismatch

A second body of evidence illustrating the lack of opportunities on a structural level is the spatial mismatch between the number of people in economically depressed geographical areas and the number of opportunities in such areas.[12] This is particularly apparent for those residing in urban inner cities or distressed rural regions. Such areas are not hard to find: the rural Mississippi delta; inner-city Cleveland, Chicago, or St. Louis; American Indian reservations across the Southwest; or the Appalachian mountain region. In these areas, economic opportunities have largely moved away (or were never there in the first place), leaving behind many scrambling for the few chairs that are left.

William Julius Wilson documented this process in his study of inner-city Chicago residents, with the book aptly titled *When Work Disappears.* Wilson stated: "The increasing suburbanization of employment has accompanied industrial restructuring and has further exacerbated the problems of inner-city joblessness and restricted access to jobs."[13] Illustrative of this is Katherine Newman's ethnography of jobs and economic conditions in central Harlem during the mid-1990s; she found that there were as many as 14 applicants for each fast-food job offered.[14]

Similarly, Cynthia Duncan described the process of diminishing jobs and opportunities in rural America, leaving behind thousands who must compete with one another for the dwindling number of viable economic opportunities. As she noted:

> *Work is hard to find. Only half the working-age men are employed, only a quarter of working-age women. "These days you can't even buy a job," complains one young man recently laid off from a mine. "Even men have a hard time getting work around here," a young single mother from Michigan explains. She was told to go on welfare when she went looking for work through the Department of Employment.*[15]

Many other areas of spatial mismatch can be found, including the deep-seated rural poverty found across the Deep South and the Mississippi delta region. This is an area with a history of slavery and cotton plantations, with many of the poor the descendants of slaves and sharecroppers. Good job opportunities are often far and few between.[16] Likewise, some of the counties in the Southwest and northern plains (including parts of Alaska) are marked by extremely high poverty. Much of this poverty is specific to Native Americans, often on reservations. These counties frequently have some of the highest rates of poverty in the country. The history here is one of exploitation, broken treaties, lack of opportunities, and the decimation of Native people. There simply are not many good job opportunities found in these areas.

What we see in these localities are many more players than chairs available. Such a mismatch is clearly visible. The historical and cultural context of each region are unique, but the lack of opportunities on a structural level is endemic to all, resulting in extremely high rates of poverty.

Life Course Risk of Poverty

Another way of thinking about the economic structural failings is to consider the lifetime risk of experiencing poverty. Rather than asking the question of how many people are poor in any given year, the question becomes: What percentage of the American population will at some point in their lives experience poverty? I would argue that a substantial percentage of Americans experiencing poverty implies an economic failure at the structural level.

The longitudinal research that I have conducted with my colleague Thomas Hirschl has helped shed light on the issue of the life course risk of poverty. Over two decades ago, we were interested in asking a very basic question: How likely is it that an American will experience poverty firsthand? Furthermore: What are the chances that an American will use a social safety net program at some point during their adulthood? In order to answer these questions, we turned to an invaluable longitudinal data set: the Panel Study of Income Dynamics, otherwise known as the PSID.

The PSID is a nationally representative, longitudinal sample of households interviewed from 1968 onward.[17] It has been administered by the Survey Research Center at the University of Michigan, and it constitutes the longest-running panel data set in both the United States and the world. The PSID initially interviewed approximately 5,000

U.S. households in 1968, obtaining detailed information on roughly 18,000 individuals within those households. These individuals have since been tracked annually (biennially after 1997), including children and adults who eventually break off from their original households to form new households (e.g., children leaving home or adults following a divorce). Thus, the PSID is designed so that in any given year the sample is representative of the entire U.S. population.

As its name implies, the PSID is primarily interested in household information about economics and demographics. For each wave of the study, there is detailed information about the annual income for each household. Consequently, one can easily determine whether households fall into poverty across the various years of the study. The survey also asks questions pertaining to whether anyone in the household has used a social safety net or welfare program at some point during the year.

Based on these data, we constructed a series of what are known as life tables. The life table is a technique for calculating how often particular events occur during a specific period of time and is frequently used by demographers and medical researchers to assess risk (i.e., the risk of having a heart attack during later adulthood). It allows one to estimate the percentage of the American population that will experience poverty at some point during adulthood.

Using this life table approach, the risk of experiencing poverty for the American population can be assessed. Results indicate that between the ages of 20 and 75, nearly 60% of Americans will experience at least 1 year below the official poverty line, while three-quarters of Americans will encounter poverty or near poverty (150% below the official poverty line). These findings indicate that a clear majority of Americans will directly experience poverty at some point during their adulthood.

Rather than a small fringe on the outskirts of society, the majority of Americans will encounter poverty. In Table 6.2 we can observe the cumulative percentages of the population who will be touched by poverty or near poverty. Between the ages of 20 and 35, 31.4% will have experienced poverty; by age 55, 45.0%; and by age 75, 58.5%. Similarly, 76.0% of the

Table 6.2 CUMULATIVE PERCENTAGE OF AMERICANS EXPERIENCING
POVERTY BY AGE

Age	Below 1.00 Poverty Line	Below 1.25 Poverty Line	Below 1.50 Poverty Line
	Level of Poverty		
20	10.6%	15.0%	19.1%
25	21.6%	27.8%	34.3%
30	27.1%	34.1%	41.3%
35	31.4%	39.0%	46.9%
40	35.6%	43.6%	51.7%
45	38.8%	46.7%	55.0%
50	41.8%	49.6%	57.9%
55	45.0%	52.8%	61.0%
60	48.2%	56.1%	64.2%
65	51.4%	59.7%	67.5%
70	55.0%	63.6%	71.8%
75	58.5%	68.0%	76.0%

SOURCE: Panel Study of Income Dynamics, Rank and Hirschl calculations.

population will have spent at least 1 year below 150% of the official poverty line by the time they reach age 75.

This pattern holds up regardless of how we might measure poverty. For example, in a complimentary analysis, we relied on a relative measure of poverty: the likelihood of Americans falling into the bottom 20% of the income distribution as well as the bottom 10%.

Table 6.3 shows the results from that analysis. We calculated that 61.8% of Americans between the ages of 25 and 60 would at some point experience at least 1 year below the 20th percentile, while 42.1% would fall below the 10th percentile.[18] Again, the likelihood of poverty was quite pronounced across the life course.

Using a broader definition of economic turmoil that includes experiencing poverty, receiving a social safety net program, or encountering a spell of unemployment results in even higher rates. Consequently,

Table 6.3 CUMULATIVE PERCENTAGE OF AMERICANS
EXPERIENCING RELATIVE POVERTY BY AGE

Age	Bottom of Income Distribution	
	20 Percent	10 Percent
30	41.6%	22.7%
35	47.7%	27.7%
40	51.2%	31.8%
45	53.9%	34.6%
50	56.5%	37.3%
55	59.1%	39.5%
60	61.8%	42.1%

SOURCE: Panel Study of Income Dynamics, Rank and Hirschl calculations.

between the ages of 25 and 60, 79.0% of the American population experienced one or more of these events during at least 1 year, and 49.8% experienced 3 years or more of such turmoil.[19]

One of the reasons these percentages are so high is that over long periods of time detrimental events are much more likely to happen, which can then throw individuals and their families into poverty. As discussed in Chapters 2 and 4, these events include losing a job, families splitting up, or medical and health emergencies, all of which have the potential to start a downward spiral into poverty. As we look across broad expanses of time, the probabilities of one or more of these events occurring increase significantly.

Our analyses also indicated that poverty is quite prevalent during both childhood and older age. Between the time of birth and age 17, 34.1% of American children will have spent at least 1 year below the poverty line, while 40.5% will have experienced poverty or near poverty (125% of the poverty line).[20] Similarly, 40.4% of the elderly will encounter at least 1 year of poverty between the ages 60 and 90, while 47.7% will encounter poverty at the 125% level.[21]

These findings suggest that given its widespread nature, poverty appears systematic to the economic structure. Occasionally, we can physically see widespread examples of this. For instance, the regions mentioned previously as marred by spatial mismatch are illustrative. Or, take the case of unemployment as described by sociologist C. Wright Mills:

> When, in a city of 100,000, only one man is unemployed, that is his personal trouble, and for its relief we properly look to the character of the man, his skills, and his immediate opportunities. But when in a nation of 50 million employees, 15 million men are unemployed, that is an issue, and we may not hope to find its solution within the range of opportunities open to any one individual. The very structure of opportunities has collapsed. Both the correct statement of the problem and the range of possible solutions require us to consider the economic and political institutions of the society, and not merely the personal situation and character of a scatter of individuals.[22]

The economic collapse during the Great Depression of the 1930s was endemic of the situation that Mills described. Given the enormity of the collapse, it became clear to many Americans that most of their neighbors were not directly responsible for the dire economic situation they found themselves in. This awareness helped provide much of the impetus and justification behind the New Deal.

In many ways, poverty today is as systematic as in these examples. Yet we have been unable to see this because we have not been looking in the right direction. By focusing on the life-span risks, the prevalent nature of American poverty is revealed. At some point during our adult lives, the bulk of Americans will face the bitter taste of poverty. The approach of emphasizing individual failings or attributes as the primary cause of poverty loses much of its explanatory power in the face of such patterns. Rather, given the widespread occurrence of economic vulnerability, a life-span analysis points to a third line of evidence indicating that poverty is more appropriately viewed as a structural failing of American society.

In short, by conceptualizing and measuring impoverishment over the adult life course, one can observe a set of proportions that truly cast a new structural light on the subject of poverty in the United States. For the majority of American adults, the question is not if they will experience poverty, but when.

Poverty Rates Across Countries

A final major structural failure can be found at the political and policy level. Contrary to the popular rhetoric of vast amounts of tax dollars being spent on public assistance, the American welfare state, and particularly its social safety net, can be more accurately described in minimalist terms.[23] Compared to other Western industrialized countries, the United States devotes far fewer resources to programs aimed at assisting the economically vulnerable.[24] As Charles Noble wrote: "The U.S. welfare state is striking precisely because it is so limited in scope and ambition."[25]

On the other hand, most European countries provide a wide range of social and insurance programs that largely prevent families from falling into poverty. These include substantial family or children's allowances, designed to transfer cash assistance to families with children. Unemployment assistance is far more generous in these countries than in the United States, often providing support for more than a year following the loss of a job. Furthermore, universal health coverage is routinely provided, along with considerable support for child care. The result of these social policy differences is that they substantially reduce the extent of poverty in Europe and Canada, while U.S. social policy has had only a small impact on poverty reduction.

An analysis of mine empirically demonstrated the impact of social policy on alleviating poverty. Using the latest data for a group of high-economy countries in the Organization for Economic Cooperation and Development (OECD), the analysis calculated the relative poverty rates (falling below 50% of median income) among these countries before taxes and social welfare programs were calculated (pretax/transfer) and after (posttax/transfer). The results are shown in Table 6.4. We can see that the average posttax/transfer poverty reduction factor among OECD countries

Table 6.4 PRETAX/TRANSFER AND POSTTAX/TRANSFER RELATIVE POVERTY RATES ACROSS SELECTED OECD COUNTRIES

Country	Pretransfer Poverty Rates	Posttransfer Rates	Poverty Reduction Factor
Iceland	16.9%	4.9%	71.1%
Denmark	24.2%	6.1%	74.8%
Finland	34.0%	6.5%	80.9%
Ireland	33.8%	7.4%	78.1%
Belgium	33.1%	8.2%	75.2%
Norway	25.9%	8.3%	68.0%
Netherlands	26.8%	8.3%	69.0%
France	37.2%	8.5%	77.2%
Sweden	24.9%	8.9%	64.3%
Austria	30.4%	9.4%	69.1%
Poland	28.5%	9.8%	65.6%
Germany	32.1%	9.8%	69.4%
Portugal	31.2%	10.4%	66.7%
Luxembourg	30.1%	11.4%	62.1%
Canada	24.1%	11.6%	51.9%
Greece	31.2%	12.1%	61.2%
Australia	25.3%	12.4%	51.0%
United Kingdom	28.0%	12.4%	55.7%
Italy	33.7%	14.2%	57.9%
Spain	34.0%	14.2%	58.2%
Average (excluding United States)	29.3%	9.7%	66.9%
United States	26.8%	17.8%	33.6%

SOURCE: OECD data, Rank calculations.

(excluding the United States) was 66.9%. The average OECD poverty rate was cut from 29.3% to 9.7%. In other words, this group of countries was able to reduce their rate of poverty by two-thirds once the effect of social policies were taken into account. The nations with the largest reduction factors were Finland (80.9%), Ireland (78.1%), and France (77.2%), leaving each with among the lowest posttax/transfer poverty rates.

Turning to the United States, the U.S. pretax/transfer poverty rate of 26.8% was slightly lower than the OECD average of 29.3%, yet it displayed the highest posttax/transfer poverty rate at 17.8%. The United States was only able to cut its rate of poverty modestly. The reason for this limited rate of reduction is that the social policies of the United States are much weaker than other OECD countries. The U.S. reduction factor is approximately half (33.6%) of the OECD average (66.9%).

A United Nations Children's Fund (UNICEF) analysis found a similar trend for child poverty rates before and after taxes and transfers. The analysis focused on 35 countries, including the United States. The average reduction in child poverty after taxes and transfers was 40% across the other 34 countries, while the United States achieved only an 8% reduction, leaving it with the second-highest posttax/transfer child poverty rate (23%) in front of only Romania (26%).[26]

A similar pattern can be found when examining pre- and posttax/transfer measures of income inequality. Economists Max Roser and Esteban Ortiz-Ospina calculated the Gini coefficients of OECD countries' pretaxes/transfers and compared them to the Gini coefficients of those countries posttaxes/transfers. The Gini coefficient is a frequently used measure of income inequality. Values fall between 0 and 1, with a value of 0 representing perfect equality, and a value of 1 representing perfect inequality. The higher the value, the more unequal the income distribution in that country. The OECD pretax/transfer Gini coefficient average (excluding the United States) was 0.47, putting the United States above average at 0.51 but not in the lead; 20 countries were in the same neighborhood (0.48 or higher), and 6 countries had Gini coefficients greater than the United States. It is after taxes and transfers where the United States stands out. The U.S. posttax/transfer Gini coefficient was 0.39, tied with

Turkey for third highest, in front of only Mexico (0.46) and Chile (0.47). The average for the other OECD countries in the analysis was 0.31.[27]

Even the risk of poverty for single-parent families, which some believe is unavoidably high, is highly dependent on the country in which it occurs. An analysis of 24 countries by Laurie Maldonado and Rense Nieuwenhuis demonstrated this. The average poverty rate for single-parent families' pretax/transfer across the other 23 non-U.S. countries in this analysis was 42%. At 49%, the United States was above average, in front of only five other countries. Yet once taxes and transfers were taken into consideration, the average single-parent family poverty rate in the other 23 countries fell from 42% to 19%. On the other hand, the United States only managed to reduce single-parent family poverty by one-third through taxes and transfers (from 49% to 33%). The authors interpreted their data to indicate that "the U.S. is still an exceptional case due to its lagging policy to address the labor market inequalities. The point being the U.S. does not have national policies for paid leave and child allowance, and provides little public expenditure on childcare and preschool—all consequential to reducing poverty."[28]

Sociologist David Brady and colleagues have shown that the United States attaches a much higher penalty to specific behaviors associated with the risk of poverty.[29] These include single parenthood, unemployment, and low educational attainment. While other countries provide support for those who fall into these categories, U.S. policy has sought to punish those who engage in this behavior by withholding economic support. The result is a much higher overall rate of poverty.[30]

Consequently, a major reason for the posttax/transfer differences in poverty and economic inequality is the level of generosity found in the social programs across these countries. As social welfare scholars Cheol-Sung Lee and In-Hoe Koo explained: "Total public expenditures on social policies and overall measures of welfare generosity are highly correlated with relative poverty" among wealthy democracies. "Critics of welfare states have questioned the effectiveness of government poverty programs" they wrote, but researchers of the welfare state have ultimately provided "more convincing evidence."[31] When countries choose to provide generous social benefits to their citizens, they tend to have less poverty and greater economic equality.

These cross-national analyses clearly illustrated a major structural failing leading to the high rates of U.S. poverty. It is a failure at the political and policy levels. Specifically, social and economic programs directed to the economically vulnerable populations in the United States are minimal in their ability to raise families out of poverty. While America has always been a "reluctant welfare state," the past 40 years have witnessed retrenchments and reductions in the social safety net. These reductions have included scaling back both the amount of benefits transferred, as well as a tightening of program eligibility.[32] In addition, the United States has failed to offer the type of universal coverage for child care, medical insurance, or child allowances that most other developed countries routinely provide. As a result, the overall U.S. poverty rates remain at extremely high levels.

Once again, this failure has virtually nothing to do with the individual. Rather, it is emblematic of a failure at the structural level. By focusing on individual characteristics, we lose sight of the fact that governments can and do exert a sizable impact on reducing the extent of poverty within their jurisdictions. In the analysis presented here, Canada and Europe were able to lift a significant percentage of their economically vulnerable above the threshold of poverty through governmental transfer and assistance policies. In contrast, the United States provides substantially less support through its social safety net, resulting in poverty rates that are currently the highest in the industrialized world.

The one area where the United States has effectively reduced the rate of poverty for a particular group has been that of the elderly.[33] Their substantial reduction in the risk of poverty over the past 60 years has been directly attributed to the increasing generosity of the Social Security program, as well as the introduction of Medicare in 1965 and the Supplemental Security Income program in 1974. During the 1960s and 1970s, Social Security benefits were substantially increased and indexed to the rate of inflation, helping many of the elderly escape poverty. Without Social Security, the elderly poverty rate in the United States today would climb from its current

10% to over 40%.[34] Kathleen Romig noted: "Social Security benefits play a vital role in reducing poverty in every state, and they lift more Americans above the poverty line than any other program."[35] A majority of American seniors (those aged 65 and older) depend on Social Security for the bulk of their income. Almost half (48%) are economically vulnerable and would be in dire straits without their Social Security income, as David Cooper and Elise Gould explained:

> *Many of America's 41 million seniors are just one bad economic shock away from significant material hardship. Most seniors live on modest retirement incomes, which often are barely adequate—and sometimes inadequate—to cover the costs of basic necessities and support a simple, yet dignified, quality of life. For these seniors, and even for those with greater means, Social Security and Medicare are the bedrock of their financial security. . . . With nearly half of all seniors in the United States falling below the threshold of economic vulnerability, policymakers must be especially careful when considering changes to the social insurance programs—predominantly Social Security and Medicare—that protect this group.[36]*

Medicare is also critically important to the economic security of American seniors. In 1963, before the implementation of Medicare, almost half (48%) of seniors were uninsured, a number that dropped to 1% by 2016. A recent analysis revealed that seniors today pay 13% of their healthcare costs out of pocket, only a quarter of what they paid in the 1960s.[37]

Once again we see the impact that social policies have on reducing poverty. These policies have the potential to increase the economic protections that individuals and families receive, thereby reducing their overall vulnerability and risk of poverty.

In each of the earlier cases, it is relatively easy to visualize the mismatch between the number of players versus the number of chairs. This mismatch illustrates the third point of the structural vulnerability explanation of poverty—given the structural failures, a certain percentage of the American population will experience economic vulnerability regardless of what their characteristics are. As in the musical chairs analogy, the game is structured such that some of the players are bound to lose. As one interviewee from my *Living on the Edge* book put it:

> *There are only so many good-paying jobs that exist in this society, and there are tons and tons of minimum wage jobs. And as long as we expect people to work them, there are gonna be people who can't make it without help. There's only so many people can rise to the top, and then no more can.*[38]

Increasing everyone's human capital will do little to alter the fact that there are only a limited number of decent-paying jobs available. In such a case, employers will simply raise the bar in terms of their employee qualifications, leaving behind a more qualified percentage of the population at risk of economic deprivation. Consequently, although a lack of human capital and its accompanying vulnerability lead to an understanding of who the losers of the economic game are likely to be, the structural components of our economic, social, and political systems explain why there are losers in the first place.

VISUALIZATION

In these last three chapters I have reviewed the major components of the structural vulnerability approach. We now can pull these elements together into an overall framework. The main components of the structural vulnerability framework are shown in Figure 6.1. The figure visually illustrates that there are two ways of understanding individual vulnerability to poverty. Paths A and B deal with the question of who is at risk of poverty in America, while paths C and D focus on the question of why poverty exists.

The bulk of the empirical research pertaining to American poverty has focused on Path A. Economists, sociologists, and demographers have concerned themselves with understanding the individual attributes that

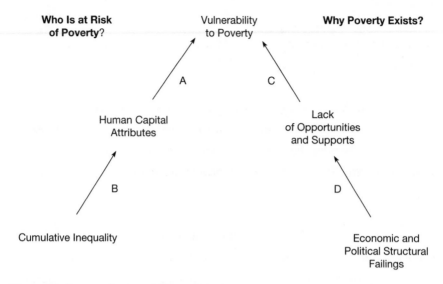

Figure 6.1 Structural vulnerability model of poverty.

are associated with a greater risk of impoverishment. As discussed, these attributes can be largely understood in terms of human capital. The lack of human capital limits an individual's ability to compete in the labor market. Consequently, those with less education, fewer job skills, health problems, and so on will face heightened vulnerability to poverty.

Path B suggests that cumulative inequality largely determines which Americans are more likely to lack such human capital. Several background characteristics are instrumental in producing cumulative disadvantage. The most important of these is social class: Those growing up in lower- or working-class families are more likely to have their acquisition of human capital assets truncated. In addition, race, gender, and differences in innate abilities also play a role in influencing the acquisition of human capital.

Paths A and B therefore explain who in America is at greater risk of experiencing poverty during their lives. The critical mistake has been the following: Poverty analysts have confused the question of who is at risk of poverty with the question of why poverty exists. They have stopped at Path A in their explanations of poverty. According to mainstream research, the question of why poverty exists is typically answered by noting that the poor lack education, skills, and so on, and that these are the reasons for impoverishment. We can see in Figure 6.1 that this is an incomplete account.

The right-hand side of the structural vulnerability model includes Paths C and D. These explain why so many Americans are at an elevated risk of poverty. Path C suggests that the lack of opportunities and social supports is a critical reason for this risk. As discussed, there is a mismatch between the number of jobs that will adequately support a family and the number of families in need of such jobs. Likewise, American society has failed to provide the necessary supports for those in need; the United States has been marked by a minimal safety net, inadequate child care assistance, lack of healthcare coverage, a dearth of affordable low-cost housing, and so on. This lack of economic opportunities and social supports has significantly raised the number of Americans vulnerable to the risk of poverty.

The shortage of opportunities and adequate supports has been produced by structural failings at the economic and political levels (Path D). The tendency of our free market economy has been to produce a growing number of jobs that will no longer support a family. In addition, the basic nature of capitalism ensures that unemployment exists at modest levels. Both of these directly result in a shortage of economic opportunities in American society.

In addition, the absence of social supports stems from failings at the political and policy levels. The United States has traditionally lacked the political desire to put in place effective policies and programs that would support the economically vulnerable. Structural failings at the economic and political levels have therefore produced a lack of opportunities and supports, resulting in high rates of American poverty. To return to our previous analogy, Paths A and B are designed to explain who is more likely to lose out at the game, while Paths C and D are intended to explain why the game produces losers in the first place.

Consequently, we can think of the dynamic of poverty as a large-scale game of musical chairs. For every 10 American households, there are good jobs and opportunities at any point in time to adequately support perhaps 8 of those 10. The remaining two households will be shut out of such opportunities, often resulting in poverty or near poverty. Individuals experiencing such economic deprivation are likely to have characteristics putting them at a disadvantage in terms of competing in the economy (less education, fewer skills, single-parent families, illness or incapacitation, non-Whites residing in inner cities, etc.). These characteristics help to explain why particular individuals and households are at greater risk of poverty.

Yet, given the previously discussed structural failures, a certain percentage of the American population will experience economic vulnerability regardless of what their characteristics are. The structure of the American economy, in consort with its weak social safety net and public policies directed to the economically vulnerable, ensure that millions of Americans will experience impoverishment at any point in time, and that a much larger number will experience poverty over the course of a lifetime. The fact that three-quarters of Americans will experience poverty or near poverty during their adulthood is emblematic of these structural level failings.

LOOKING AHEAD

In the next three chapters, I apply the structural vulnerability model to a wider context. Addressing the dynamics we have been discussing in the structural vulnerability framework is consistent with several important principles and values. These are discussed in Chapter 7.

In Chapter 8, I use the structural vulnerability model to help guide the types of policies necessary to address and alleviate each of the pressure points in the overall model. A range of strategies is discussed. Finally, in Chapter 9 I look briefly to the past and point to the future in order to argue that a structural vulnerability understanding can effectively lead to a significant reduction in poverty.

PART III

The Broader Context

Building the Foundation

Values underlie all social policy. The foundation of any policy or program is built on a set of values and beliefs. As we shall see in the Chapter 8, understanding poverty from the perspective of structural vulnerability implies particular policies for alleviating poverty. But it also suggests a specific set of values that those policies are embedded in. In this chapter we explore these values.

Such an examination is important in garnering support for the policies outlined in Chapter 8. If we can agree on the importance of particular values, and if we can show that these values are being undermined by the processes described in the structural vulnerability model, then we can begin to make strong arguments for the necessity of particular policies to reduce poverty.

REVISITING THE MODEL

Let us return to the model diagramed in Chapter 6. Figure 7.1 displays the specific values promoted by addressing the factors in each of the pathways shown. As discussed in Chapter 4, the lack of human capital helps to explain who is at greater risk of experiencing poverty (as shown in Path A). The value behind investing in human capital is the importance of maximizing human potential. By increasing the level of human capital, individuals are able to live fuller and more enriching lives. In

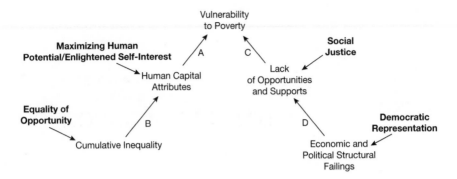

Figure 7.1 Structural vulnerability model with underlying values.

addition, maximizing human capabilities creates the potential for a more dynamic and productive society. This reinforces the value of enlightened self-interest.

Path B indicates that cumulative inequality leads to lowered levels of human capital. In particular, social class differences result in differences in education, skills, and abilities. The value that underlies reducing cumulative inequality is the importance of equality of opportunity. The United States has long emphasized the belief that everyone is entitled to certain opportunities in order to make their way through life. Cumulative inequality undercuts this value by producing a very uneven playing field.

Path C specifies that a major reason for poverty is the lack of opportunities and supports. As discussed previously, there is a shortage of decent-paying jobs for all in need of such work. In addition, the social safety net in the United States is extremely weak, offering little protection to households experiencing economic insecurity. These are conditions that lay beyond the control of individuals. The United States is also the wealthiest country in the world, with the ability to address these shortcomings. The fact that it does not is a case of social injustice. It is simply unfair and unjust that so many suffer needlessly in a country with the resources that the United States has.

Finally, Path D signifies that failings at the economic and political levels result in this lack of opportunities. In particular, programs and policies that provide adequate support for the disadvantaged are weak. This partially reflects an absence of the disenfranchised within the political decision-making process. This lack of input from lower income households is the result of a failure of democratic representation for all in society. Too often it is the interests of the privileged that are disproportionally represented. By addressing the concerns and needs of the less advantaged, the democratic system can move toward better representing those who have been traditionally ignored.

MAXIMIZING HUMAN POTENTIAL/ENLIGHTENED SELF-INTEREST

In earlier work, I discussed the importance of achieving what I and others have referred to as a "livable life."[1] A livable life can be thought of as one in which an individual is able to thrive and develop in a healthy manner across their lifetime in order to reach their full potential. One of the ways in which individuals are able to achieve such a life is through cultivating human capital. Investments in education and skills can result in individuals more fully developing their talents and abilities. This can clearly facilitate a fulfilling life.

While it is clear from Figure 7.1 that human capital by itself does not explain why poverty exists, investing in an individual's human capital is nevertheless smart social policy. One can argue that such investments have a positive effect on the nation as a whole, resulting in a more dynamic and innovative society. This sense of a broad awareness of the benefits of such investments can be referred to as enlightened self-interest.[2] In other words, by becoming aware of the benefits of investing in our human resources, we all gain as a result. Likewise, when we fail to invest in our human potential, we suffer the consequences.

Alexis De Tocqueville referred to this in his 1840 treatise on America as self-interest properly understood.[3] In fact, the full title of the chapter from his *Democracy in America* book is "How the Americans Combat Individualism by the Doctrine of Self-Interest Properly Understood." His basic premise was that "one sees that by serving his fellows, man serves himself and that doing good is to his private advantage."

The example of poverty illustrates this principle. The cost of poverty and its repercussions for those impoverished is high. Substantial research has documented that poverty exacts a heavy toll from those who fall within its grasp.[4] To take but one example, poverty has been shown to exert a powerful influence on an individual's physical and mental health. Those living in poverty tend to have significantly worse health as measured by a variety of indicators when compared to the nonpoor.[5]

The effect of poverty on children is particularly destructive.[6] Poverty serves to stunt children's physical and mental development. Poor infants and young children in the United States are far more likely to have lower levels of physical and mental growth (as measured in a variety of ways) than their nonpoor counterparts.[7] As children grow older, and if they continue to reside in poverty, the disadvantages of growing up poor multiply, as discussed in Chapter 5. These disadvantages include attendance at inferior schools, conditions associated with poverty-stricken neighborhoods, unmet health needs, and a host of other hardships.

The result is that poverty exacts a heavy toll on the poor, making it much more difficult to lead a fulfilling life. However, what is less obvious are the economic costs of poverty to the nation as a whole.[8] To a large extent we have failed to recognize that poverty and its attendant conditions place enormous economic, social, and psychological costs on the nonpoor as well as the poor. These costs affect us both individually and as a nation, although we have been slow to recognize them. Too often the attitude has been: "I don't see how I'm affected, so why worry about it?"

Yet the issues that many Americans are in fact deeply concerned about, such as crime, access and affordability of healthcare, race relations, or economic productivity, to name but a few, are directly affected and exasperated by the condition of poverty. As a result, the general public winds up paying a heavy price for allowing poverty to walk in our midst. A report by the Children's Defense Fund on the costs of childhood poverty made this strikingly clear:

The children who suffer poverty's effects are not its only victims. When children do not succeed as adults, all of society pays the price: businesses are able to find fewer good workers, consumers pay more for their goods, hospitals and health insurers spend more treating preventable illnesses, teachers spend more time on remediation and special education, private citizens feel less safe on the streets, governors hire more prison guards, mayors must pay to shelter homeless families, judges must hear more criminal, domestic, and other cases, taxpayers pay for problems that could have been prevented, fire and medical workers must respond to emergencies that never should have happened, and funeral directors must bury children who never should have died.[9]

Yet for many Americans, poverty is seen as an individualized condition that impacts exclusively on that person, their family, and perhaps their neighborhood. Rarely do we conceptualize a stranger's poverty as having a direct or indirect effect on our own well-being. By becoming aware of such impacts through informed knowledge, we begin to understand that reducing poverty is very much in our enlightened self-interest.

A question that should be asked is, what exactly is the economic cost of poverty? An analysis by Michael McLaughlin and myself sought to estimate the annual cost of childhood poverty in the United States.[10] In order to do so, we relied on the latest government data and social science research in order to calculate the economic impact that childhood poverty exerted on the country as a whole. In particular, we examined the direct effect that childhood poverty has on lowering future economic productivity, higher healthcare and criminal justice costs, and increased expenses as a result of child homelessness and maltreatment. These costs are shown in Table 7.1.

By summing together these expenses, our overall estimate was that, in 2015, childhood poverty in the United States was costing the nation $1.03 trillion a year. This number represented 5.4% of the U.S. annual gross domestic product.

Perhaps a better way of gauging the magnitude of the costs of childhood poverty is to compare it with the total amount of federal spending in 2015.

Table 7.1 ANNUAL COST OF CHILDHOOD POVERTY

Type of Cost	Dollar Amount (in Billions)
Reduced earnings	294.0
Increased street crime victimization costs	200.6
Increased health costs	192.1
Increased corrections/crime deterrence costs	122.5
Increased child homelessness costs	96.9
Increased social costs due to incarceration	83.2
Increased child maltreatment costs	40.5
Total cost of child poverty	1,029.8

SOURCE: McLaughlin and Rank calculations.

The federal government spent a total of $3.7 trillion in 2015. This included the entire range of programs and agencies supported by the government, including defense spending, Social Security, infrastructure, and so on. The annual cost of childhood poverty—$1.03 trillion—therefore represented 28% of the entire budget spent by the federal government in 2015.

Consequently, to argue that we pay a large economic price for having the highest rates of poverty in the industrialized world is actually an understatement. Childhood poverty represents an enormous drain on both the U.S. economy and society as a whole. It results in sizable losses in economic productivity, higher healthcare and criminal justice costs, and significant costs associated with remedial efforts to address the fallout of childhood poverty.

Poverty stunts the ability of individuals to build their human capital. As Martin Ravallion noted: "Children growing up in poorer families tend to suffer greater human development gaps, with lasting consequences for their adult lives."[11] Impoverished children grow up with fewer skills and are less able to contribute to the economy. They are more likely to engage in crime and experience more frequent healthcare problems. These costs are ultimately borne by not only the children themselves, but also the wider society as well. By investing in the human capital of those who are lacking in such resources, they have a greater chance of reaching their potential. This, in turn, benefits the entire society.

EQUALITY OF OPPORTUNITY

The concept of equality in America is an interesting one. It has seldom been thought of in the sense that every American should experience equality of outcomes. Rather, it has meant that there should be equality in terms of access to opportunities.[12] Every citizen has the right to an education, good health, and a means to a livelihood. No one should be denied these on the basis of income, race, gender, or other extraneous factors.

Furthermore, equality of opportunities includes the notion that individuals be judged and rewarded on the basis of their abilities. Political philosopher John Rawls defined fair equality of opportunity as "Those who are at the same level of talent and ability, and have the same willingness to use them, should have the same prospect of success regardless of their initial place in the social system, that is, irrespective of the income class into which they are born."[13]

The process of cumulative inequality as diagramed in Path B of Figure 7.1 undercuts this value. As described in Chapter 5, the playing field for American children is most certainly uneven. Some are starting out with clear advantages, while others are beginning with obvious disadvantages. These then tend to multiply over time. This process of cumulative inequality undermines and erodes the value of equality of opportunity. The analogy of an altered game of Monopoly was used to illustrate this unevenness.

One person I interviewed for my *Chasing the American Dream* book witnessed this process hundreds of times. Chris Johnson occupied a unique position in which to observe these patterns. On the one hand, he held the position of a professor at an elite university, where many of his students were children of privilege. On the other hand, he had worked and interacted with inner-city, poverty-stricken African American children over the past 30 years. During this time he founded and developed a studio designed for inner-city kids to learn about the process of creating their own art in a workshop located in an extremely distressed section of town. He had seen firsthand the process of both cumulative advantage and disadvantage. As Chris explained in our interview:

> *You know partly it's just history, sort of, the domino falling into the present. I think we create these kind of closed loops, the Billie Holiday song, "Them that's got, gets more." I think opportunity leads to opportunity, and lack of opportunity leads to lack of opportunity. So what happens is some people, because of things outside of their control, are ill prepared to take advantage of something or maybe they never get a chance to take advantage of something, and then that becomes the prerequisite for the next thing. And that becomes the prerequisite for the next rung. So initial opportunity or initial lack of opportunity becomes critical.*
>
> *Obviously a child born into an intact family with a college fund already waiting for them with good nutrition and a safe environment and terrific schools is going to have a whole different outcome than someone born in the projects to a single mom on crack with lousy schools and drug dealers outside.*
>
> *And I think this is also what angers me is that people don't realize how hard it is if you're born with all that against you, this headwind, how hard it is to move up compared to someone who's got a tailwind just helping them along.[14]*

In other work, I have used the example of bicycling with or against the wind to illustrate this.[15] When one is cycling with the wind, you do not feel anything at all, and yet it is helping to push you along. It is quite easy to think that you are having a great day with much strength and power. It is only when you turn into the wind that you realize the force of the wind that several minutes ago had been quietly helping you to propel ahead. Similarly, those with advantages often take them for granted, not realizing the full impact that they are having.

Such wide differences in resources during childhood ensure that there is inequality of opportunities. The argument here is that inequality of outcomes actually leads to inequality of opportunity. By addressing widespread cumulative inequality, we are strengthening the principal of equality of opportunity.

SOCIAL JUSTICE

In the past, I have written about the concept of justice within the context of poverty.[16] In a nutshell, justice within the context of the United States has come to imply a sense of fairness and deservedness. For example, when someone works hard and plays by the rules, we often hope that they will receive their "just rewards." On the one hand, when a crime is committed, justice is seen as being served if the criminal is sentenced to a punishment that fits the nature and severity of the crime. On the other hand, if an individual commits a serious crime and is neither apprehended nor punished, the feeling is that an injustice has occurred.

Thus, in cases where individuals experience outcomes and consequences that are congruent with their prior actions and behaviors, the world is seen as just. Conversely, in situations where individuals experience outcomes and consequences that are incongruent with their prior actions and behaviors, the world is perceived as unjust.

This concept of balance can be visually seen in the symbol of justice found from local courtrooms to the U.S. Capitol: that of Themis or Lady Justice. Here one finds a woman, often blindfolded, holding a measuring scale in one hand and a sword in the other. Justice is portrayed as being impartial and not beholden to special interests (hence the blindfold). The fact that she is holding the scales has a double meaning. They first imply that evidence should be weighed carefully in deciding how justice will be delivered. But they also connote that justice is served by balance. That is, prior actions and future consequences should be in balance and congruent with one another. Furthermore, the sword gripped in her right hand represents the strength and authority of justice and acts as a balance to the judgment derived from the scales held in her left hand.[17]

If we think of justice in terms of balance and congruence, we can ask whether the condition of poverty is just. Poverty is clearly a negative condition that very few people would wish on themselves. Consequently, the critical question becomes: Is such poverty deserved as a result of prior negative actions and behaviors? If the answer is yes, justice in the above sense is served. If the answer is no, an injustice has occurred.

This has been the criterion used over the centuries, particularly since the English Poor Laws of 1601, to divide the poor into the categories of deserving and undeserving.[18] As discussed in Chapter 3, the deserving poor are individuals deemed worthy of our compassion and assistance because they find themselves in poverty through little fault of their own. Thus, an injustice has occurred. Such persons would include those who suffer from an unavoidable illness or accident, children, widows, and so on. On the other hand, individuals falling into the undeserving poor category are seen as meriting neither our compassion nor our assistance. Such poverty is perceived as being brought about as a result of laziness, immorality, or some other failing, and therefore impoverishment is a just or deserving consequence of prior behavior.

Using the above concept of justice, to what extent is poverty just? My argument would be that for the vast majority of individuals in poverty, the condition is quite unmerited and therefore unjust. As we have seen in previous chapters, poverty is largely the result of failings at a structural level. To hold individuals responsible for such structural failures makes little sense. Or to put it another way, the condition of poverty is most certainly not deserved.

However, there is another way of thinking about justice, and that is on a societal level. The United States is a wealthy country. Despite the ongoing concerns about the federal debt, we have the ability to prioritize our goals in order to make a vigorous effort to reduce poverty by providing greater opportunities and supports to lower income families. However, we largely choose not to do so. As a result, we live in a society where an injustice is occurring for the vast majority of the poor, yet collectively we choose to look the other way.[19]

In order to make the United States a more socially just society, the necessary opportunities and supports should be provided. A social justice lens requires us to eliminate the paradox of poverty amid prosperity. This was precisely the contrast that President Johnson was referring to in his inaugural address of 1964, when he spoke about the meaning of America:

> *Conceived in justice, written in liberty, bound in union, it was meant one day to inspire the hopes of all mankind; and it binds us still. If we keep its terms, we shall flourish. First, justice was the promise that all who made the journey would share in the fruits of the land. In a land of great wealth, families must not live in hopeless poverty. In a land rich in harvest, children just must not go hungry. In a land of healing miracles, neighbors must not suffer and die unattended. In a great land of learning and scholars, young people must be taught to read and write.*[20]

To allow such situations to exist on a societal level violates one of our most fundamental principles—that of justice.

DEMOCRATIC REPRESENTATION

Path D in Figure 7.1 specifies that failure at the economic and political levels results in a lack of opportunities and supports for lower income households. This failure reflects the fact that the concerns and interests of those with fewer resources are often neglected in American society and its political players. Yet in a democracy, the interests of all groups should be well represented in the policy process. That is, government should be "of the people, by the people, and for the people." By its very definition, a democracy implies that all citizens and groups have equal access and representation in the democratic process. The true nature of a democracy is attained through such access, participation, and representation.[21]

This process can be thought of in terms of a level playing field. As Thomas Simon wrote:

> *All definitions of democracy have a common presupposition. All pre-*
> *suppose a level playing field. The phrase "a level playing field" serves as*
> *a convenient metaphor for saying that a democracy, defined anyplace*
> *along the spectrum, presupposes the absence of a wide disparity in the*
> *participatory capabilities of the citizenry. Widespread participatory*
> *disparity, especially among groups, undermines democracy.*[22]

Thus, where particular groups tend to be excluded or underrepresented from democratic participation (for whatever reasons other than voluntary), there is a structural flaw in the democracy.

Poverty, I would argue, reflects one of those structural flaws. Impoverishment significantly impacts on the poor's ability to fully participate in the democratic process.[23] For example, the act of voting is systematically made more difficult for the poor. Although this right exists for all, economic deprivation disproportionally blocks the full realization for those who fall within poverty's ranks. The fact that the United States conducts its elections on Tuesdays rather than on weekends, combined with our cumbersome registration procedures, tends to create barriers for the poor. Leonard Beeghley noted:

> *In sum, while any individual can presumably go to the polls, the struc-*
> *ture of voting means that middle-class and rich people dominate this*
> *form of participation. The poor and working class are least capable*
> *of voting on a working day, getting registered, coping with voting*
> *procedures, and overcoming the problem posed by separate and fre-*
> *quent elections. These facts exist externally to individuals, decisively*
> *influencing rates of participation. Thus, for those at the lower end of*
> *the stratification hierarchy, the pluralist system may seem open but it*
> *is closed in fact.*[24]

Other aspects of democratic participation are also made more difficult for those in poverty. For instance, the ability to lobby and exert influence on the appropriate players is often critical in the democratic decision-making process in today's America. Such lobbying efforts are highly dependent on financial resources, of which the poor by definition have little. Thus, the poor's "special interests" are rarely lobbied for in the same manner and with the same economic clout that other special interest groups are able to engage in. As a result, the concerns and needs of the poverty stricken are frequently given short shrift in the public arena.[25]

Likewise, the ability to be well informed regarding pertinent issues is an important component of democracy.[26] Wise decision-making on both an individual and collective basis derives from citizens being able to understand the various facets and dimensions of particular topics and then to act on such knowledge. Poverty compromises the ability of low income households to have such understanding, which in turn affects the quality of their participation. Less education, coupled with fewer resources and ongoing concerns with economic survival, often result in the poor not being as informed regarding public issues as the rest of society.

As a result of the above tendencies, the poor are often invisible to the democratic process. A poignant expression of this was voiced at the beginnings of the country by John Adams:

> *The poor man's conscience is clear; yet he is ashamed. . . . He feels himself out of the sight of others, groping in the dark. Mankind takes no notice of him. He rambles and wanders unheeded. In the midst of a crowd, at church, in the market . . . he is in as much obscurity as he would be in a garret or a cellar. He is not disapproved, censured, or reproached; he is only not seen.*[27]

This sense of darkness and obscurity captures the essence of the poverty stricken being left out of the democratic process.

In short, the democratic process is undermined by the existence of poverty. Economic deprivation infringes on the ability of individuals to participate in the same manner as others within society.[28] Such disparities should raise a red flag among those who believe in the importance of democracy. As Simon argued: "It does not make any sense for a nation to proclaim itself a democracy if there is widespread and structural participatory disparity within the nation. A nation that strives for democracy must make a commitment to alleviate the plight of disadvantaged groups."[29] Addressing the economic and political structural failings begins to recognize the interests of the less fortunate in society. By doing so, American democracy can become more representative of all its citizenry.

The structural vulnerability model diagramed in Figure 7.1 illustrates the dynamics and causes of poverty. But it also suggests that by addressing these factors, a set of key values can be reinforced. These include maximizing human potential, enlightened self-interest, equality of opportunity, social justice, and democratic representation. I would argue that a general agreement can be built around the importance of strengthening these values and principles. The structural vulnerability approach for addressing poverty does just that. The model also points the direction with respect to policies that can alleviate poverty. We turn now to several of these policies.

Policy Implications

A major reason for the historically high rates of poverty in the United States is that our social and economic policies aimed at poverty alleviation have been largely ineffective or minimal. And a key reason for why they have been ineffective or minimal is because they have been based on the traditional American understanding of poverty discussed in Chapter 3. The relevant analogy would be that of a doctor who has misdiagnosed their patient. No matter how high a dosage of the wrongly prescribed medicine, it is unlikely to be effective and in fact may prove to be harmful. Such has been the case with poverty.

Our policies have been primarily aimed at attempting to "improve" individuals such that they either can make their way out of poverty or are able to avoid poverty in the first place. From this perspective, the causes of poverty are viewed as lying within the attitudes and behavior of the individual, and specifically, that there is some type of individual failing that needs to be corrected. Therefore, the solutions to poverty must lie with reforming or improving the individual or simply letting them work through their shortcomings on their own.

This tactic has taken several different forms. One approach has been referred to as "tough love." This strategy is closely associated with various welfare reform measures over the years. It has included a variety of incentives and disincentives, carrots and sticks, to entice individuals to "do the right thing." Particular behaviors, such as giving birth, are disincentivized, while other behaviors, such as locating a job, are incentivized.[1]

A second major approach aimed at improving individuals is through job training and skill development programs. The goal of these programs is to make poverty-prone individuals more competitive in the labor market. These programs target improving the skills of individuals such that they are able to locate and secure better-paying jobs.[2]

A third major policy approach has been one of benign, or not so benign, neglect. This is premised on the belief that government programs do more harm than good; therefore, social policy should be kept to a minimum in the lives of the populace.[3] Indeed, the social safety net in the United States has often been referred to as the "reluctant welfare state." None of these approaches has been very effective because they have failed to address the underlying causes of poverty.

Let us return to our structural vulnerability model of poverty, now shown in Figure 8.1. As in the prior chapter, we can use this model to help guide what policies and strategies will effectively alleviate poverty. The model implies that there are four points of effective policy intervention, each dealing with a different element in the process. Path A was discussed in Chapter 4 and represents the fact that individuals lacking in human capital are at a greater risk of poverty. As we discussed in Chapter 7, maximizing human potential underlies the strategy of increasing access to key public resources. We focus on three components of this strategy: providing quality and accessible education; healthcare; and housing.

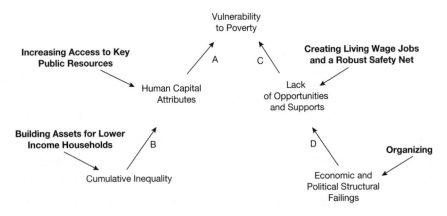

Figure 8.1 Structural vulnerability model with poverty alleviation strategies.

Next, Path B in Figure 8.1 was discussed in Chapter 5. A major reason for the lack of valuable human capital has to do with growing up in lower income households. As a result, the ability to build one's human capital is more constrained. This clearly violates the principle of equality of opportunity discussed in Chapter 7. In order to address this imbalance, asset-building policies are discussed designed to improve the opportunities for those from a more disadvantaged background.

In Chapter 6, we discussed both Paths C and D in Figure 8.1. The root cause of poverty is that there are simply not enough opportunities and supports for all in society, as shown in Path C. Addressing this builds on the value of social justice. Two key strategies are discussed: increasing the number of livable wage jobs and providing a robust safety net to protect individuals from falling into poverty.

Finally, Path D indicates that the reason for the lack of opportunities and supports has to do with failings at the economic and political levels. These failings reflect the failure of our democratic system to represent all of its people. In order to exert pressure on these structures, the strategy of organizing is highlighted. In each of these cases, I simply touch on several policy strategies that are necessary. Greater details and specifics behind implementing these strategies can be found in the wide array of research and policy briefs cited in the notes.

INCREASING ACCESS TO KEY PUBLIC RESOURCES

I begin with the importance of increasing access to key public resources. In some respects, the conditions of poverty and near poverty in the United States are worse than the actual dollar amounts would indicate. The reason is that several key social and public goods have become increasingly inaccessible for a number of American households. In particular, a quality education, healthcare, and affordable housing either are out of reach or are obtained only through considerable economic expenditure and hardship. Yet these social goods are vital in building and maintaining healthy and productive citizens.

Virtually every other Western industrial society provides greater access and coverage to healthcare and affordable housing than does the United States.[4] They also do not display the wide fluctuations in educational quality that American children are subjected to at the primary and secondary levels. Why? The underlying reason is the belief that there are certain social and public goods that all individuals have a right to, and that making such resources accessible results in more productive citizens and societies in both the short and long run. There is also the recognition that they reduce the harshness of poverty and inequality.

In addition, while the lack of human capital is not the root cause of poverty, it is nevertheless the case that those lacking in such skills and abilities may be unable to take advantage of particular job and other opportunities that become available. Investing in a society's human capital can also lead to a more innovative and productive workforce, which in turn may create more job opportunities in the future.

Quality Education

The ability to receive a quality education is one of the most vital assets that an individual can acquire. Indeed, a key motivation behind the introduction of public education in the mid-1800s was the importance of making education accessible to the general public, rather than only the wealthy and privileged. Horace Mann, the well-known 19th century educator, spoke of public education as the "great equalizer" and as a place where both disadvantaged and advantaged children would be taught under one roof. The expansion and access to public education has had a profound impact on the well-being of Americans and American society. It has contributed to an effective and productive workforce, a more informed citizenry, and countless other benefits.

Public education remains the avenue through which most Americans acquire their educational training. The vast majority of today's students attend public schools. In 2021, 90% of all primary and secondary students were enrolled in public schools, while 74% of students going on to college attended public institutions.[5] As a result, public education is the dominant vehicle for the vast majority of American students.

Unfortunately, as a result of the way that public education is funded at the primary and secondary levels, the quality of that education varies widely depending on the wealth of the community where one resides.[6] As discussed in Chapter 5, the bulk of U.S. school funding for elementary, middle, and high schools comes from the local tax base, primarily property taxes. Well-to-do school districts with a richly endowed property tax base will generally have ample funding to operate quality public schools. This involves paying teachers competitive salaries, keeping student/teacher ratios low, purchasing the necessary educational resources (e.g., books for libraries or computer equipment for instruction), and so on.

On the other hand, residing in a poor community with a diminished tax base often results in schools that are financially strapped. Teachers are frequently underpaid and overstressed, the physical facilities may be severely deteriorated and outdated, and class sizes are often quite large, along with a host of other disadvantages. These children, who are predominantly low income and frequently of color, wind up being denied a quality education as a result. Linda Darling-Hammond and Laura Post wrote:

Few Americans realize that the U.S. educational system is one of the most unequal in the industrialized world, and students routinely receive dramatically different learning opportunities based on their social status. In contrast to most European and Asian nations that fund schools centrally and equally, the wealthiest 10 percent of school districts in the United States spend nearly ten times more than the poorest 10 percent, and spending ratios of three to one are common within states. Poor and minority students are concentrated in the less well funded schools, most of them located in central cities and funded at levels substantially below those of neighboring suburban districts.[7]

As a result, many of these children receive an inferior education, which in turn will dramatically reduce their ability to effectively compete in the labor market.

To deny children the fundamental right to a decent education is both morally wrong and bad social policy. Countless studies have documented the immediate and lingering effects of high-quality versus inferior-quality education on later life outcomes.[8] Improving public education for low income children is absolutely essential.

It is clear that although money in and of itself is not the complete answer, it nevertheless represents a large part of the solution. This is particularly the case for school districts unable to provide the necessary educational tools for its students (qualified teachers, educational materials, etc.). Evening out the vast financial differences currently found across school districts and then spending the additional money wisely by hiring qualified teachers and building strong curricula can make a significant difference. As Craig Jerald, a senior policy analyst at the Education Trust put it: "The picture has become crystal clear. If you do both of those things you can really solve the problems."[9]

Emphasis should be placed on the federal and state governments to even out the gaping disparities in school financing. Several states have begun to move in this direction, but many more need to follow their lead. As noted above, differences in spending per pupil can vary by thousands of dollars, with wealthy students who are blessed by myriad social and economic advantages enjoying the most in terms of public per pupil spending, while students from poor backgrounds and possessing the fewest advantages wind up receiving the least in terms of public tax dollars.

Healthcare

As with education, access to quality healthcare is often dependent on the size of one's wallet. For those who can afford it, America offers some of the finest medical care in the world. Yet for those unable to absorb the increasing costs, they are frequently left out in the cold without healthcare. As a result, too many Americans are finding themselves lacking health insurance, with insufficient coverage, or with adequate coverage but only at a considerable expense. As sociologist Ronald Angel wrote: "The United

States is unique among developed nations in not providing a basic package of health care to all of its citizens."[10]

A major reason that the United States has failed to provide universal access to health insurance is that healthcare coverage has not been understood as a basic human right.[11] In virtually every other industrialized country, having access to healthcare is viewed as a basic right. With the exception of the elderly, the United States has not accepted this premise.

In 2021, 27.2 million Americans or 8.3% of the population lacked health insurance throughout the year. For those below the poverty line, 16.2% had no health coverage in spite of the Medicaid program.[12] Furthermore, if we look across a several year period, we find that many more Americans are without healthcare at some point.[13] And for too many Americans with health insurance, the deductibles may be high and the coverage itself sorely lacking.

The passage of the Affordable Care Act (ACA), and its signing into law by President Obama in 2010, has had a strong effect on reducing the number of Americans without health coverage. The law's major provisions went into full effect in 2014, and since then the number of uninsured has been cut approximately in half.[14] More Americans are able to access the health system through the ACA than ever before. Nevertheless, the United States still does not offer the kind of universal healthcare coverage found in virtually all the other Organization for Economic Cooperation and Development (OECD) countries.

One of the reasons that many Americans lack healthcare coverage, particularly those in or near poverty, is that their place of work does not provide healthcare coverage. Since World War II, the United States has primarily tied health insurance to one's job. Until the 1970s, this worked reasonably well, but as discussed in previous chapters, an increasing number of low wage and part-time jobs have been created during the past 40 years, with many of these jobs lacking health benefits.[15] Furthermore, for those under age 65 but out of work, health coverage is unlikely except through the Medicaid program.

Access to healthcare is important in a variety of ways. Being able to address one's health needs is crucial in maintaining a productive life, both at work and at home. What then can be done to increase the healthcare access for those who find themselves left out?

The issue of reforming healthcare is enormously complex, as was demonstrated in the documentation of the 2010 ACA, which ran over 1,000 pages.[16] The legislation reflected the power of various interest groups (e.g., the insurance industry, the American Medical Association, etc.) to shape the particular healthcare changes. However, what is now needed is to build a system around the fundamental principle of universal coverage. As noted, the United States is far and away the exception among the industrialized countries in not offering universal coverage for its citizens. The question is not whether we have the funds to spend on healthcare. In fact, we spend more than any country on a per capita basis or as a percentage of gross domestic product (GDP).[17] Rather, the question is how best to spend these resources in order to ensure that all Americans will have access to healthcare while maintaining the overall quality of the system. Universal coverage is essential in reforming the current healthcare system.

Affordable Housing

Affordable housing represents a third key public good that has become harder to come by in recent years, particularly for low income households.[18] The general rule of thumb is that households should spend no more than 30% of their income on housing (which is the standard definition of affordable housing). Yet, the Joint Center for Housing Studies at Harvard University estimated that for low income renters, slightly over 70%, were severely burdened by their rental costs, while an additional 10% were moderately burdened.[19]

One of the reasons for this has been that the cost of housing over the past 40 years has risen much more steeply than that of worker's wages. For example, the National Low Income Housing Coalition estimated that in order to afford the fair market rent for an average two-bedroom apartment (i.e., paying 30% of one's income for rent), a worker needs to be earning \$25.82 an hour.[20] Yet as we have seen previously, many heads of households are earning well below this. Wages have stagnated over the past 50 years after taking inflation into account, and the economy has been producing more jobs at the lower end of the wage scale. For example, the median wage of a retail sales worker in 2022 was \$14.59 per hour, which is clearly insufficient to afford the rent on a two-bedroom apartment or to purchase a median-priced home in any major metropolitan area.[21]

Furthermore, particular areas in the United States have a much more severe shortage of affordable housing than the national average. In the state of Massachusetts, one needs to be earning \$33.81 an hour to be able to rent an adequate two-bedroom housing unit, while in the city of San Francisco \$60.96 an hour is needed.[22] As the Millennial Housing Commission noted:

> *There is simply not enough affordable housing. The inadequacy of supply increases dramatically as one moves down the ladder of family earnings. The challenge is most acute for rental housing in high cost areas, and the most egregious problem is for the very poor.*[23]

In addition to the proliferation of low wage work, the private sector's failure to build an adequate stock of lower-end housing units, coupled with the federal government's decreasing expenditures on programs designed to address the housing needs of low income families, have made affordable housing even scarcer over the past 30 years. The result is that more Americans, particularly those in the bottom quintile of the income distribution, are finding themselves without access to decent-quality affordable housing. Given these patterns, it is no wonder that homelessness has become such a visible issue over the past four decades.

In order to strengthen the access that low income Americans have to decent-quality affordable housing, two basic approaches are called for. The first is through the building of lower cost housing, and the second is through providing housing vouchers that make it easier for lower income families to acquire housing.

There is a clear need to increase and strengthen the country's stock of affordable and modestly priced housing. Both new construction and renovation of existing housing stock should to be undertaken. Tax incentives can be strengthened to encourage the private market to build and renovate existing housing stock (e.g., the Low Income Housing Tax Credit of 1986), and where private construction is not feasible, the federal and state governments need to become more directly involved in housing construction.

A second venue for increasing the accessibility of affordable housing to lower income households is through the expansion and more effective use of housing vouchers. Currently there are approximately 2.2 million households using Section 8 housing vouchers in the country.[24] The program is designed to allow families with low income to rent private housing on the open market from those landlords who will accept the vouchers and whose rental units qualify for the program. Individuals pay no more than 30% of their income toward their rent, with the government making up the difference.[25] The program has generally been considered a success in opening up the housing market to lower income families. It allows individuals some flexibility and movement in terms of their housing decisions. Unfortunately, it has become increasingly difficult for families to find landlords who are willing to accept the vouchers. Policies should be put in place to encourage and increase landlord participation, as well as modifying the program to expand and strengthen it.

Each of the initiatives in this section is designed to help individuals realize their full potential. Access to quality education, healthcare, and housing provides a solid foundation for being able to develop one's talents and skills. They also enable individuals to compete for a wider variety of jobs and occupations in the labor market.

BUILDING ASSETS FOR LOWER INCOME HOUSEHOLDS

Turning back to Figure 8.1, we can see in Path B that cumulative inequality impacts on the acquisition of human capital. One of the reasons for this pertains to the wide differences in assets and resources across socioeconomic status. Consequently, policies that build the assets of lower income households can facilitate their ability to acquire valuable human capital and to be able to transfer those assets from one generation to the next.[26] The acquisition of assets can therefore allow individuals from more disadvantaged economic backgrounds to gain ground in the future and, for our purposes, reduce their risk of poverty. Assets build a stake in the future that income by itself often cannot provide.[27] Unfortunately, the opportunities to acquire such assets have been in short supply for lower income individuals.

The asset policies discussed here are guided by the belief in equality of opportunity (as discussed in Chapter 7). A number of policies are in place that encourage asset accumulation for the middle and upper classes. Yet, for those from lower economic backgrounds, such opportunities are often not available.[28] It is only fair that comparable policies be developed for those with fewer resources. As Thomas Shapiro and Edward Wolff observed: "Current public policy offers substantial, highly regressive subsidies for wealth and property accumulation for relatively well-off individuals. In contrast, poverty policy has ignored asset building for resource-poor families."[29] The policies suggested here are an attempt to redress this imbalance.

There have been periods in our history when social policy was explicitly designed to foster asset accumulation for a large number of Americans, including those at the lower end of income distribution (although racial groups such as African Americans and American Indians have been routinely excluded). For example, the Homestead Act of 1862 allowed pioneers to lay their stake on 160 acres of land. As long as they remained and worked the land for 5 years, they became its owners. This policy enabled many families to build their future and their children's future. During the 75-year duration of the Homestead program, 1.5 million households were given title to 246 million acres of land.[30] In addition, the homestead itself represented a very tangible asset that could then be handed down to the next generation. By the time of the fourth generation, it is estimated that approximately 46 million Americans were descendants and beneficiaries of those who had homesteaded. The Homestead Act constituted a major asset-based policy in U.S. history that improved the

lives of millions and played an important role in the economic development of the United States.

Another large-scale asset based policy was the GI Bill. Initiated in 1944,
the original GI Bill provided $500 dollars per year for college tuition and
$50 dollars a month for living expenses to veterans of World War II. This
policy had a profound impact on opening the doors of higher education to
those who were without such help. At its peak in 1947, 49% of all students
enrolled in higher education were supported by the GI Bill. Nearly 8 million World War II veterans received educational benefits provided by the
bill. In addition, approximately 10 million veterans of World War II and
the Korean War were able to use the GI loan program to purchase homes
or start businesses.[31] Once again, not only did this policy help millions of
Americans, but also it was a sound investment in the country as a whole.[32]

Although not as dramatic as the above examples, policies continue to
exist that encourage the development of assets. These policies are primarily delivered through the tax code (known as tax expenditures). For example, the ability to deduct the interest paid on a home mortgage when
filing one's income tax returns has enabled millions of Americans to lower
their costs of owning a home. Partially as a result of this, the home has
come to represent a major asset held by many Americans.[33] Clearly, governmental policy has encouraged the accumulation and growth of home
ownership. Other examples of asset-building policies through the tax
code include the lower tax rate on capital gains, the deduction allowed
for contributions to individual retirement accounts (IRAs), and the exclusion of employer contributions to pension funds. However, each of these
types of asset policies primarily benefit the middle and upper classes. It is
estimated that 75% of such tax expenditures go to families in the top 40%
of the income distribution, while 24% go the top 1%.[34]

The rising tide of children's development accounts (CDAs) is an important asset-building policy for households at the lower end of the income
spectrum.[35] These accounts are designed to build the savings of children
such that the savings can be used for educational or other expenses when
the children turn 18. These are generally started with an initial deposit by
the government when the child is born, and then later deposits by parents

are frequently matched by state governments. These programs are found in a majority of U.S. states as well as in a number of other countries.

Children's development accounts can be structured such that lower income families receive a higher dollar match from the state. When children reach the age of 18, the CDAs can then be used to help fund the pursuit of a degree beyond high school. By doing so, they enable lower income young adults to build their skills and expertise and therefore increase their overall human capital.

Another idea for asset building is expanding programs that enable Americans to build up their personal savings so they can provide rainy-day protection. Many states around the country have been experimenting with such policies. They allow individuals to put aside a percentage of their monthly income with a generous match from the state, in much the same way that employers contribute to employees' 401(k) accounts. These funds can then be used to address future concerns and expenses. Ramping up such a policy on a federal level could provide an important reservoir for families in need.

An additional means of developing assets and broadening the base of wealth is through employee ownership plans. These include employee stock ownership plans, 401(k) plans, and broad-based stock option plans. Data from the General Social Survey indicated that, as of 2014, 19.5% of all employees working in the private sector reported owning stock or stock options in their companies.[36] Employee ownership plans represent another potential means for individuals to build their assets while raising the productivity of workers. An example of a country that has invested heavily in the concept of asset building has been Singapore, with its Central Provident Fund (CPF). Introduced in 1955, the CPF is a mandatory pension fund in which its members are able to use their savings for housing, medical expenses, and education.

The idea of economic reparations is yet another asset-building tool to be considered. As William Darity and Kristen Mullen argued, the case for reparations to U.S. Black descendants of slavery is a strong one.[37] In an analysis looking at the White/Black wealth gap from 1860 to 2020, Ellora Derenoncourt and colleagues found the gap in 1860 was 60 to 1, but this fell to 10 to 1 by 1920. However, from the 1950s onward the closure of the gap has stalled, remaining at 6 to 1 over the past 70 years.[38] The historical patterns of slavery and discrimination have resulted in Black Americans possessing much less wealth than their White counterparts. The authors wrote: "The main reason for such a large and lasting gap is the enormous difference in initial wealth between Black and white Americans on the eve of the Civil War. . . . Our long-run view of the racial wealth gap underscores the importance of slavery and postslavery institutions for the persistence of the wealth gap."[39] A policy of reparations would begin to address the historic and ongoing wrongs that have been committed to African Americans.[40] The monetary reparations might be structured in a way that could be used to build Black Americans' assets, including attaining a higher education, providing a down payment on a home, or starting a small business.

INCREASING THE AVAILABILITY OF LIVING WAGE JOBS

Referring to Figure 8.1, we can now focus on Path C. From a policy perspective, there is a clear need to address the lack of opportunities and supports in society. Essential to this strategy are policies that will increase the availability of jobs that can support a family to live above the poverty line. As economist Bradley Schiller argued: "Jobs—in abundance and of good quality—are the most needed and most permanent solution to the poverty problem."[41]

The problem of not enough jobs has played itself out somewhat differently within an American versus a European context. Within the United States, the economy over the past 50 years has done quite well in terms of creating new jobs. The problem has been that many of these jobs are low paying and/or lacking in basic benefits such as healthcare.[42] The result is that although unemployment rates have been relatively low in the United States (often averaging between 4% and 6%), working full-time does not ensure that a family will be lifted out of poverty or near poverty. For example, Timothy Smeeding and colleagues found that 25% of all American full-time workers could be classified as being in low-wage work (defined as earning less than 65% of the national median for full-time jobs). This was by far the highest percentage of the high-economy countries analyzed, with the overall average falling at 12%.[43]

In contrast, European economies have been more sluggish in terms of creating new jobs over the past 50 years, resulting in unemployment rates much higher than in the United States. In addition, workers have remained out of work for longer periods of time. However, for those who are employed, employees are generally paid more and have greater benefits than their American counterparts, resulting in substantially lower rates of poverty.

What then can be done to address the related problems of jobs that do not pay enough to support a family and the problem of not enough jobs in the first place? Two broad initiatives would appear essential. The first is transforming the existing job base so that it is better able to support families. The second is the creation of enough jobs to employ all who are in need of work.

Within the context of the United States, one might begin with the following benchmark: Individuals who are employed full time throughout the year (defined as working 35 hours per week over a 50-week period) should be able to generate earnings that will enable them to lift a family of three above the near poverty threshold (150% of the poverty line). Such a family might include a married couple with one child, a one-parent household with two children, or a three-generation household of mother, grandmother, and son. The 2021 near poverty threshold for a family of three in the United States was set at $32,339. Consequently, in order to lift such a family above the poverty line, an individual needs to be earning approximately $18.50 an hour.

There are two specific ways of accomplishing this. One is to raise the minimum wage to a level that will support a family so it is above the near poverty line, and then index the wage to inflation so that it will continue to lift such a family over the poverty line in the future. A second approach is to provide a tax credit (e.g., the Earned Income Tax Credit [EITC]) that supplements workers' wages so that their total income for the year lifts them above the poverty line.[44]

The minimum wage in the United States went into effect in October 1938 at an initial level of $0.25 an hour. The basic concept was that no employee should fall below a certain wage floor. There was an underlying value that workers should receive a fair wage for a fair day's work. However, unlike Social Security, the minimum wage has never been indexed to inflation; changes in the minimum wage must come through congressional legislation. Years go by before Congress acts to adjust the minimum wage upward, causing it to lag behind the rising cost of living. The current minimum wage in the United States stands at $7.25 an hour, a rate that went into effect in July 2009. An individual working full time at the minimum wage during the year (50 weeks at 35 hours per week) would earn a total of $12,688, far short of the $32,339 needed to lift a family of three above the near poverty line.

As noted, to lift such a family above the near poverty line an individual needs to be earning at least $18.50 per hour. Consequently, what is needed is to raise the minimum wage to $18.50 per hour, and then index it each year to the rate of inflation in order to hold its purchasing power. The phase-in period to raise the minimum wage to $18.50 per hour might take place over several years in order to spread out the increase. Indeed, many states currently have a minimum wage much higher than the federal minimum wage.

The positive impact of tying the minimum wage to the near poverty level for a family of three and indexing it to the rate of inflation would be substantial. First, it would establish a reasonable floor below which no full-time worker would fall. Second, it would allow such a worker to support a family of three above the poverty line. Third, it would reinforce the value that Americans have consistently attached to work. Fourth, it would remove the political wrangling from the minimum wage debate. Fifth, it would address in a limited way the increasing inequities between chief executive officers who earn 300 times what their average paid workers earn.

A second approach for supplementing and raising the earnings of low-income workers is through the tax structure, specifically through the use of tax credits. The primary example of such a credit in the United States is the EITC. The EITC was enacted in 1975 and underwent a significant expansion during the 1990s. It currently represents the largest cash antipoverty program in the United States and is frequently considered one of the more innovative American economic policy ideas.

The program is designed to provide a refundable tax credit to low income workers, with the vast majority of the credit going to households with children. For 2021, a family with one child could qualify for the EITC if its earned income was below $42,158 (or $48,108 for married couples), while a family with three or more children could qualify if its household income was under $51,464 (or $57,414 for married couples). The maximum credit for a one-child family was $3,618; the benefit rose to $6,728 for a family with three or more children. The credit is normally received in a lump-sum payment as part of an overall tax refund for the previous year. Since it is a refundable credit, families receive the payment even if they do not owe any taxes.

The goals of the EITC are to deliver economic relief at the low end of the earnings distribution and to furnish a strong work incentive. An individual cannot qualify for the EITC without earned income, and the impact is particularly strong at the lower levels. For example, for a head of household with one child and earning $7.50 an hour (and the total earnings were under $10,000), the EITC would effectively raise her wage by an additional $3.00 an hour to $10.50 an hour.

The program thus provides a significant supplement to low earners as well as an incentive to work. In 2018, it was estimated that 28 million Americans benefitted from the EITC, and along with Child Tax Credit, pulled approximately 10.6 million individuals above the poverty line who otherwise would have fallen into poverty.[45] For families that remain in poverty, the EITC has helped to reduce the distance between their household income and the poverty line. It has also enabled families to purchase particular resources that can improve their economic and social mobility (i.e., school tuition) or to meet daily expenses.

In order to make the EITC even more effective, its benefits should be expanded so that they provide greater assistance to low income workers without children. The vast majority of the EITC benefits go to families with children. Yet there is no compelling reason why such benefits should not also be provided for individuals without children (although they were raised modestly for 2021). Further research also needs to be done in order to examine the feasibility of receiving the EITC throughout the year, rather than as lump sum during the tax season. Third, some households that qualify for the EITC fail to claim and take advantage of the tax credit. Better educating tax filers about the benefits of the EITC appears warranted. Finally, state EITC programs should be encouraged as an additional antipoverty component on top of the federal EITC benefits.

The policy of an expanded EITC, in conjunction with the raising and indexing of the minimum wage to the level of a living wage, would substantially help working women and men in the United States who, in spite of their efforts, are unable to get themselves and their families out of poverty or near poverty. In addition, such policies begin to address (although in a very limited way) the increasing inequalities and perceived unfairness of the American income distribution and wage structure.

In terms of the problem of producing enough jobs, in many ways this is a much more difficult task than supplementing and raising the wages of existing jobs. Nevertheless, it is essential that a sufficient number of jobs be available to meet the demands of the existing labor pool.

Various labor demand policies have the potential to generate a more robust rate of job growth. Several approaches can be taken. First, economic policy should seek in a broad way to stimulate job growth. This would include fiscal policies such as increasing government expenditures, enhancing tax incentives for investment, or enacting consumer tax cuts. The strategy of investing in a "Green New Deal" could be one specific area of such investment.[46] Monetary policy can also provide a stimulus by making access to credit easier and cheaper.

A second approach is to provide targeted wage subsidies to employers in order to stimulate job creation. Although the details of such programs can vary considerably, the basic concept is that an employer receives a monetary subsidy for creating a position and/or hiring an individual (often from a targeted population) that the employer might not have created without such an incentive. This approach could be aimed at businesses and industries that are potential employers of individuals from lower income or lower skill backgrounds.

A third strategy for generating jobs is through public service employment. As David Ellwood and Elisabeth Welty noted in their review of the effectiveness of public service employment programs, if done carefully and judiciously, they can help increase employment without displacing other workers, and they can produce genuinely valuable output.[47] Such an approach appears particularly pertinent for those out of work for long periods of time.

Taken as a whole, an overall strategy for reducing poverty must begin with a set of policies that will increase the availability of jobs that can economically support families so they can live above the poverty threshold. To a large extent, poverty is the result of not having a job or having a job that is not able to viably support a family.

PROVIDING AN EFFECTIVE SOCIAL SAFETY NET

Another important strategy for addressing the lack of opportunities and supports found in Path C in Figure 8.1 is the building of a robust and effective social safety net. No matter how strong economic growth and job creation may be, many individuals and families will periodically fall between the cracks. Whether through the loss of a job, a sudden disability, or some other unanticipated event, there are times and situations in people's lives when a social safety net is needed.

The economist Hyman Minsky pointed out that free market economies are prone to periods of instability, such as periodic recessions and economic downturns. Safety net programs help to serve as automatic stabilizers for the economy during these periods.[48] That is, they grow during times of need and diminish during more prosperous times. For example, as rates of unemployment rise, more individuals draw on unemployment insurance to weather the temporary economic problems caused by a lack of jobs. As economic conditions improve, more people are able to find jobs and so no longer need unemployment insurance. In this fashion, safety net programs help to automatically stabilize the instability inherent within the economy.

A social safety net is therefore important in assisting individuals and families during times of need and in alleviating the economic instability associated with recessionary periods. One of the reasons that the United States rate of poverty is so high and the Scandinavian nations are so low is a result of differences in the extent and depth of their social safety nets. As discussed in previous chapters, compared to other Western industrialized countries, the United States devotes far fewer resources to programs aimed at assisting the economically vulnerable. In fact, the United States allocates a smaller proportion of its GDP to social welfare programs than virtually any other industrialized country.

In contrast, most European countries provide a wide range of universal social and insurance programs that largely prevent families from falling into poverty. These include substantial family or children's allowances that are designed to transfer cash assistance to families with children. Unemployment assistance is far more generous in these countries than in the United States, often providing support for more than a year following the loss of a job. Furthermore, health coverage is routinely provided, along with considerable support for child care.[49]

The result of these social policy differences is that they substantially reduce the extent of poverty in Europe and Canada, while U.S. social policy exerts a smaller impact on poverty reduction. As we saw in Chapter 6, government transfers had a significant effect on reducing poverty among a variety of OECD countries. Rebecca Blank noted: "The national choice in the United States to provide relatively less generous transfers to low-income families has meant higher relative poverty rates in the country. While low-income families in the United States work more than in many other countries, they are not able to make up for lower governmental income support relative to their European counterparts."[50]

Consequently, a key reason behind why the United States has such high levels of poverty is a result of the nature and scope of its social safety net. The United States provides substantially less support to its social safety net than other countries, resulting in poverty rates that are currently among the highest in the industrialized world. As Lane Kenworthy argued:

> *The United States has done less well by its poor than a number of other affluent nations. The reason is straightforward. Like their counterparts abroad, America's least well-off have been hit hard by shifts in the economy since the 1970s, but whereas some countries have ensured that government supports rise as the economy grows, the United States hasn't.*[51]

One strategy for providing a more robust safety net is to strengthen the current array of social welfare programs. This might be accomplished through better coordination across the various programs as well as investing greater resources into providing the needed services that they provide.

An alternative policy strategy that approaches a social safety net in a substantially different manner is what is known as a universal basic income. The concept itself has been proposed at various times across the past few centuries. In fact, Thomas Paine, the author of *Common Sense* in 1776, was an early proponent of a guaranteed income for all Americans.

The basic structure would be that every citizen in the United States is guaranteed a set amount of income from the government. This income would be received on a monthly or bimonthly basis. All would be entitled to this income, regardless of whether they were employed or not. Advocates argue that such an approach is a straightforward and effective way of addressing poverty: Since poverty is a lack of income, providing a guaranteed minimal income can substantially reduce poverty directly. In addition, the argument is made that this represents a possible solution to a future in which automation and artificial intelligence are likely to dominate the workplace. On the other hand, opponents point to potential work disincentives embedded in such a program.

The United States seriously considered the idea of a guaranteed income in the early 1970s, with President Richard Nixon proposing to Congress a variant of this idea. Currently, several countries have been exploring the feasibility of such a policy, most notably Finland and Switzerland. In addition, the idea has been gaining some traction within the progressive wing of the Democratic Party.

For example, Democratic candidate Andrew Yang made it the focal point of his 2020 bid for the presidency. Yang proposed giving all U.S. citizens over the age of 18 a guaranteed payment of $1,000 per month or $12,000 for the year. He argued that such assistance would dramatically cut the rate of poverty.

The state of Alaska since 1976 has in fact had a form of a universal basic income through the Alaska Permanent Fund. Each resident receives an annual dividend derived from the oil revenue produced in the North Slope. In 2022, this amounted to $3,284.[52]

There have been a number of experiments and trials that have sought to examine the feasibility and effects of a universal basic income.[53] What these studies have generally found is that increasing the amount of income to poverty-stricken families makes a significant difference in the well-being of children and parents. As Jeff Madrick wrote, recent research

> *has increasingly shown that low income itself is key, and arguably the major cause of the debilitating outcomes in cognition, emotional stability, and health for poor children. The countless studies reinforcing this claim are an important breakthrough. . . . Now we know that there is growing evidence that universal cash transfers, money itself, can solve or mitigate many problems.*[54]

Consequently, programs that direct additional income to such families see significant gains in the physical and mental well-being of children and adults.

The concept of a child cash allowance is a similar idea. Throughout most European countries, families with children under 18 receive a monthly cash payment. This applies to all children, regardless of their circumstances. The idea behind this policy is that parents with young children are in need of additional economic help in raising their children, and that such assistance also allows parents to spend more time with their children.

From July 2021 to January 2022, a form of a child allowance went into effect in the United States. As part of the pandemic relief package, the child tax credit was amended such that most families with children under 18 were provided a monthly cash benefit of up to $300. All families with incomes below $150,000 were eligible. It was estimated that child poverty was cut by up to 45% as a result, and that when it was discontinued, child poverty increased by 41%.[55]

Advocates hope that such an amended child tax credit can be reinstated in the future. President Biden has proposed an extension, and Democrats would like to make it permanent. In doing so, it would represent a significant social policy change. As New Jersey Senator Cory Booker noted: "It's the most transformative policy coming out of Washington since the days of FDR."[56]

ORGANIZING

Finally, Path D in Figure 8.1 indicates that the lack of opportunities and supports in society is the result of failings at the economic and political levels. Free market capitalism has simply not produced enough economic opportunities for all in society. In addition, there has been a failure at both the national and state levels for public policy to address the needs of individuals in the bottom of the income distribution.[57] An important way to change these shortcomings is to exert pressure on political actors and parties through effective organizing.

Organizing can take place in a wide variety of settings, from local issues of concern in the community to unionization in the workplace, there are many avenues for bringing people together in order to exert pressure for change.

Labor Unions and Unionization

Labor unions represent one important way in which workers have been able to gain better pay and benefits. The basic idea is that in order to partially correct for the power imbalance between employers and employees, a union representing the rights of workers is necessary. The purpose of such a union is to protect its members, through what is known as collective bargaining, and by negotiating for healthy working conditions and livable wages and benefits.

Labor unions began in the United States toward the end of the 19th century and reached their zenith during the 1950s. At that time approximately one-third of all workers were represented by a union. Since then, union membership has steadily fallen, such that only 6% of workers in the private sector are currently unionized.[58]

One of the reasons for this decline has been that much of the unionized segment of the economy has traditionally been located in the manufacturing sector. As we have seen, many of these jobs have dried up as we moved from a manufacturing-based economy to a more service-based economy. In addition, unionization has been under attack from both private industry and the federal government.[59] Nevertheless, unions are still active in the United States, particularly in public sector work such as government jobs, teaching, and city employees.

Research has shown that unions can have both a direct and an indirect effect on reducing poverty. The direct effect is through increasing the wages and benefits for workers in specific low-paying occupations. These increased wages have been able to pull households above the poverty threshold. In addition research has shown that in localities with a heavier presence of organized labor, the wages for those in nonunion jobs are also raised. This effect is the result of nonunion employers needing to remain competitive in attracting qualified employees. In order to do so, they may offer higher wages and benefits than they might otherwise have offered in the absence of a union presence.

In addition, there are indirect effects that unions have on reducing poverty. Much of this is through the lobbying efforts of organized labor to influence antipoverty legislation such as minimum wage laws and greater coverage of healthcare. For example, in "many European nations, powerful labor movements helped establish and subsequently enlarge and protect generous welfare states."[60]

Indeed, countries with higher levels (70% to 80%) of unionization (e.g., Finland, Denmark, and Sweden) have lower rates of poverty, whereas countries with low rates of unionization (e.g., the United States) tend to have higher rates of poverty. This pattern also holds when looking at individual states within the United States.

Furthermore, higher levels of unionization have been shown to have a moderating effect on overall economic inequality. The rise of inequality in the United States over the past 50 years is partially attributed to the decline of unions during this same period.[61]

Consequently, one important area of organizing is centered on the workplace. Workers in unionized jobs tend to have higher wages and benefits than their counterparts in similar types of nonunionized work. Organized labor has also been instrumental in helping to support the various living wage and minimum wage campaigns that have taken place in various municipalities and states across the country, thereby improving the conditions for all lower income workers.[62]

Social Movements

A second approach to organizing is to work toward creating a social movement focused on reducing poverty and inequality. Such an effort obviously involves considerable effort, but such wide-scale action is possible. One can point to many recent movements that have arisen to address various problems. For example, the environmental movement has gathered considerable momentum in the past few decades. The growing concern about climate change and environmental degradation has resulted in many groups organizing to help reverse these trends.

The Black Lives Matter movement is another example of individuals coalescing and organizing around a topic of concern. The police and criminal justice brutalities occurring to African Americans has led to a widespread social movement to end such atrocities.

In a similar fashion, the growing number of Americans at risk of poverty and economic instability could be a focal point for a new social and economic movement. We saw glimpses of this with the Occupy movement, which captured the attention of many with its focus on the 1% and 99%. It is likely that, in the future, more Americans will be facing economic uncertainty, thereby increasing the visibility of the issue.

Social movements have the ability to change the very culture of a society. As Edwin Amenta and Francesca Polletta wrote in their review of social movements:

The enduring impacts of social movements are often cultural. Movements change the way we live and work. They make some behaviors socially inappropriate and others newly appealing. They create new collective actors, alter lines of social cleavage, and transform what counts as expertise.[63]

However, it must be recognized that there are at least two unique obstacles that hinder the ability of those in or near poverty to organize. The first is that there remains a considerable amount of stigma and shame connected with being poor. Individuals in poverty generally do not want to be identified as such. For many people, it is a mark of economic failure. This undermines the ability of the poor to think collectively and to organize around the issues of poverty and inequality. As Frances Fox Piven and Lorraine Minnite wrote:

No matter their hardship, before people can mobilize for defiant collective action, they have to develop a proud and angry identity. They have to go from being hurt and ashamed to being angry and indignant. In the 1930s, many of the jobless tried to hide their travails; hangdog unemployed workers swung empty lunch boxes as they strode down the street so the neighbors would not know. But many of the unemployed also harbored other ideas, half-formed perhaps, about who was to blame for their plight. When those ideas were evoked they could be rallied to rise up with others in anger over their condition.

They continued:

Time and again in history even the poor have found the outrage to proclaim not only that their hardships are not of their own making, but that they themselves by their defiance can compel action to alleviate those hardships.[64]

Consequently, as we have seen in previous chapters, there is a need to show that poverty is by and large a failure at the structural level. With such an understanding, individuals may be more likely to transfer their personal pain into positive collective action. Such action can potentially exert pressure on the status quo in order to create necessary and constructive change.

A second obstacle to organizing on the issue of poverty is that those who are poor or near poor generally do not have the time or resources to expend on such an effort. Individuals are often just trying to survive on a day-to-day basis, making it difficult to be concerned about issues beyond one's immediate needs. However, it is also true that the vast majority of the poor will be in poverty for only a relatively short period of time. Therefore, while they may not have the ability to focus on organizing opportunities in the present, they may have such an ability in the future.

When individuals effectively organize themselves in groups devoted to specific issues of concern, much can be accomplished. Such groups can be found in a wide array of settings, including local communities, places of worship, student groups, national organizations, and so on. Many examples exist of grassroots organizations that are working on issues with the potential to increase opportunities at the structural level, including groups focusing on living wage campaigns, child and healthcare legislation, affordable housing, and asset-building initiatives.[65]

At the same time, what is needed is a national focus on the issues of poverty and economic inequality. These are topics that underlie and pull together many of the concerns that various groups are attempting to redress. Building coalitions across racial and gender lines, socioeconomic classes, community boundaries, and various interest groups is essential for developing a strong political focus on the problem of poverty. Poverty is not an issue of "them," but rather an issue of "us." It is a problem that will affect most Americans in one way or another. Understanding this and acting politically on such information is critical. As Paul Rogat Loeb observed:

> *The lesson here is not to stop challenging injustices that arise from people's particular identities and backgrounds. But to promote human dignity, we need to build coalitions that are as broad as possible. In addition to the important task of staking out rights for specific marginalized groups, we also need to organize around issues that affect everyone, such as the unprecedented gap between rich and poor, the corrupting influence of unaccountable wealth, the threats to our environment, and the general sense of powerlessness that pervades America today.*[66]

SUMMARY

The approach of structural vulnerability provides a rough blueprint for addressing poverty via social policy and action. In order to effectively reduce poverty, policies should be targeted at each of the four points in the model. By doing so, it is possible to significantly reduce the extent of poverty and dramatically improve the lives of individuals. This chapter reviewed strategies to help relieve these points of pressure. They have included providing access to key public resources, building assets for lower income households, increasing the number of living wage jobs, strengthening the social safety net, and organizing for social change. In combination, they offer great potential for alleviating and substantially reducing poverty in America.

To summarize, policies can be designed to help both those who are most likely to experience poverty and to ameliorate the conditions that lead to poverty in the first place. The structural vulnerability model provides an understanding into this holistic approach for poverty alleviation.

Moving Forward

As I wrote at the beginning of this book, *The Poverty Paradox* has been quite some time in the making. Much of my academic career over the past decades has focused on the conditions of poverty and inequality. Throughout these years, an ongoing focus has been to develop a deeper understanding of why poverty exists and persists in the United States. The paradox of poverty amid prosperity has been both puzzling and concerning.

And yet in some ways it is not quite so puzzling. Since its beginnings, America has been steeped in the belief of rugged individualism. We as Americans have routinely sought to understand the world around us through such a lens. Social problems such as poverty are often reduced to individual pathology and failure. As a result, the country has often provided little support and opportunities to the poor, focusing instead on remediation and "tough love" solutions. Not surprisingly, these have done little to reduce the extent of poverty in the United States.

This emphasis on individual attributes as the primary cause of poverty has at times also been reinforced by social scientists engaged in poverty research. As the social survey has become the dominant methodological approach during the past 75 years and multivariate modeling being the preferred statistical approach, the research emphasis has increasingly fallen on understanding poverty and welfare dependency in terms of individual attributes. The unit of analysis in these studies is by definition the individual rather than the wider social or economic structures, resulting

in statistical models of individual characteristics predicting individual behavior. Consequently, the long-standing tension between structural versus
individual approaches to explaining poverty has largely been tilted within
the empirical poverty research community toward that of the individual.
As historian Alice O'Connor wrote:

> *That this tension has more often been resolved in favor of the individu-*
> *alist interpretation can be seen in several oft-noted features in poverty*
> *research. One is the virtual absence of class as an analytic category, at*
> *least as compared with more individualized measures of status such*
> *as family background and human capital. A similar individualizing*
> *tendency can be seen in the reduction of race and gender to little more*
> *than demographic, rather than structurally constituted, categories.*[1]

Certainly there have been social scientists who have employed a more
structural lens to understand poverty. Several of these approaches were
discussed in Chapter 3. But by and large, poverty researchers have utilized
a handful of demographic and household characteristics to model the occurrence of poverty.

What I have argued throughout this book is the need for a more struc-
turally based understanding of American poverty. The structural vulnerability approach provides us with a road map that stands apart from the
traditional ways of addressing poverty.

This approach is very much steeped in the sociological tradition of understanding the world. My background, education, and training has been
that of a sociologist. One of the best analogies I have come across describing
the sociological approach is from Kai Erikson, in which he wrote:

> *Imagine that you are walking down a sidewalk at rush hour in*
> *New York. You pass thousands of people in the space of a few moments,*
> *all of them intent on their own personal errands, absorbed in their own*
> *private thoughts, making their own individual way through the crowd.*
> *Every face is different. Every gait is different. It is difficult to sense*
> *any pattern or order in that scene, for what the eye sees down there at*

ground level is an immense scatter of individuals who are moving to their own rhythms and living out their own lives.

Imagine, however, that you climbed to the twelfth floor of a building nearby and looked down on that same sidewalk. At that elevation, you are too far away to see the expression on those faces, too far away to make any guesses about the motives that impel those people along their individual paths. From that vantage point, the eye sees a mass of humanity in motion, a swarm of particles that weave in and out as if moving along invisible tracks. A hundred thousand persons may pass down that thin strip of pavement in a matter of minutes without so much as a single collision, flowing in currents that no one seems award of. And if you are looking for drama in that scene, it may occur to you that you are witnessing a remarkable act of coordination. The movement on the sidewalk seems patterned, governed by rules, choreographed; and the wonder of it is that no one down there can tell you how the trick is done.[2]

So it has been with poverty. We have sought to understand the poor as a group of isolated individuals, rather than recognizing the social forces and processes that have pushed them into impoverishment.

Certainly individuals make decisions and choices in their lives. But these are best understood within the context of the structural processes I have discussed across these chapters. If we step back from the ground level, we are able to observe the powerful forces and currents that tend to push people in particular directions. This book has been about bringing those forces to light.

A GROWING UNDERSTANDING

As I have noted in recent work, I believe we may be on the cusp of a significant shift in our understanding of poverty, from that of individual failing to one of structural and systemic failure.[3] During the past 10 years, there has been a growing awareness and concern regarding the issue of economic inequality and hardship broadly defined. Beginning with the Occupy movement in 2011 and 2012, considerable discussion has taken place around the concept of the 1% and 99%.[4] This rising tide of discourse has also washed into mainstream political debates across the country. Presidential candidates on the progressive side of the aisle routinely discuss the alarming trend of growing income and wealth inequality in the United States.

The Black Lives Matter movement has cast a further spotlight on racial inequality in the United States, while the Fight for $15 struggle has garnered support for lifting the incomes of low-wage workers. In addition, cities and states have been raising their minimum wages in recognition of the need to assist those in low-paying jobs.

Community groups around the country have also been raising their voices to draw attention and action to the conditions of poverty in the United States. For example, the Poor People's Campaign began with Martin Luther King's call for a "revolution of values" and a march on Washington, D.C., in 1968 to seek economic justice for those in poverty. Today, the group Poor People's Campaign: A National Call for Moral Revival continues this struggle by organizing individuals and groups across the country in order to exert pressure on legislators and policymakers to address the conditions of poverty and economic hardship.

Also encouraging has been the Biden administration's emphasis on addressing some of the structural causes of poverty and inequality, rather than simply redressing individual shortcomings. A case in point was the child tax credit, which provided families with children a monthly cash benefit of up to $300 a month from July 2021 to January 2022. The Urban Institute estimated that this policy along with other measures of the American Rescue Plan Act of 2021 would have the effect of reducing the overall rate of poverty as measured by the U.S. Supplemental Poverty Measure in 2021 from 13.7% to 7.7%.[5] The bottom line is that well targeted and executed government programs can have a major effect on reducing poverty. Although conservative members of Congress have prevented most of these measures from permanently passing into law, there appears to be growing support among moderates and progressives for such policies.

Another encouraging development with the potential to increase opportunities for more Americans is the focus on rebuilding the social infrastructure of low-income Americans. This includes investing and upgrading the country's housing stock, modernizing public schools, and opening access to good quality child care. As discussed in the last chapter, the United States is clearly an outlier among the industrialized nations when it comes to providing these essential social goods for all of its citizens. In recognizing the importance of the social infrastructure, federal resources can be redirected to attack the structural failings found in today's society.

And as mentioned, a broad coalition of progressive politicians is increasingly advocating for policies that will address some of the structural and systemic failings of the economy and society. Ideas such as a universal basic income and universal healthcare coverage are being seriously weighed and considered.

So, the good news with respect to altering the country's understanding of poverty and inequality is that there has been a solid start in the last 10 years. There is a growing recognition that poverty and inequality are problems rooted at the economic and policy levels, rather than simply at the individual level. As such, there is momentum to consider more fundamental changes in our policy approaches to solving poverty. Nevertheless, there are many miles to go before such a realization becomes a consensus.

LOOKING BACK, LOOKING AHEAD

But, there is another fundamental change that must also come with this new understanding. What is now needed is a moral shift in how poverty is viewed. Just as we look back in amazement at the human conditions we once tolerated, so, too, must we realize that no one should suffer from the ravages of poverty. I believe there will come a time when we view impoverishment in such a light.

For most of my career, I have taught a course focusing on the conditions, causes, and cures of poverty in America. As a result, I have had the privilege to interact and converse with hundreds of students deeply interested in alleviating this blight on our social and economic landscape.

One of the concerns that is routinely raised by my students is the slow pace of social and policy change regarding poverty. I too share in this concern, but as I have noted, I am also cautiously optimistic that we may be on the verge of seeing substantial progress in the years ahead.

However, there is another way of thinking about such change. And that is to take the long view. I am often reminded of Dr. Martin Luther King's observation that the arch of the moral universe is long, but that it bends toward justice.[6] I believe this is true. Although it sometimes feels as if we have taken one step forward and two steps back given the current state of affairs, over the long run I would argue that the United States has become a more socially just society. Vast changes have taken place in the legal structures that now prevent the kinds of discrimination and social injustices that took place not many decades ago.[7]

Likewise, our policies and programs have gradually recognized the importance of economic protections for vulnerable groups in society. While we still lag behind many other countries, we have slowly strengthened our safety net, particularly for seniors, over the past century. I would argue that across our entire history we have made gradual progress toward the goal of economic justice.

On the eve of America's entrance into World War II, President Franklin Delano Roosevelt introduced the concept of the four freedoms in his State of the Union Address on January 6, 1941. According to Roosevelt, they represented the freedoms that America and the free world stood for: freedom of speech, freedom of worship, freedom from want, and freedom from fear. Freedom from want expressed the idea that Americans should be free from the type of poverty that we have discussed throughout this book, and as historian Eric Foner noted, this freedom seemed to "strike the deepest chord in a nation just emerging from the Great Depression."[8] Once the United States entered the war, Roosevelt's four freedoms quickly became a most important criteria for distinguishing between the Allies and the Axis, while Norman Rockwell's painting of the four freedoms was an enormously popular portrayal on the home front.[9]

Roosevelt further elaborated on the importance of freedom from want in what he referred to as a Second Bill of Rights, introduced during his State of the Union Address on January 11, 1944. The president argued that just as the first Bill of Rights protected certain liberties and rights, so too must a second Bill of Rights protect individuals from poverty.

> We have come to a clear realization of the fact that true individual freedom cannot exist without economic security and independence. "Necessitous men are not free men." People who are hungry and out of a job are the stuff of which dictatorships are made.
>
> In our day these economic truths have become accepted as self-evident. We have accepted, so to speak, a second Bill of Rights under which a new basis of security and prosperity can be established for all—regardless of station, race, or creed.[10]

Roosevelt proposed that such a Bill of Rights include having a job that pays a livable wage; being able to own a home; having access to adequate medical care and the opportunity to achieve and enjoy good health; the right to a good education; the right to protection from the economic fears of old age, sickness, accident, and unemployment; among others. This represented a shift in thinking toward understanding basic human rights, and it led to the "Universal Declaration of Human Rights" adopted by the United Nations in 1948. In addition, President Harry Truman, in his 1945 and 1949 addresses to Congress, sought to build on Roosevelt's economic proposals through a multiple-point program of legislative action.

These proposals are as relevant today as they were 75 years ago, if not more so. Roosevelt, Truman, and the United Nations recognized that freedom from poverty must be a basic human right. They also recognized that poverty diminishes us all. In a land of plentiful resources and prosperity, economic destitution should not exist. It is simply wrong. The time has come to acknowledge and accept this basic understanding of the world we live in. The structural vulnerability framework detailed throughout this book provides a jumping off point for this understanding.

As some have noted, history does not always move toward a more progressive or enlightened future. Sometimes we move backward before moving forward. Since the 1980s, our progress toward alleviating poverty has stalled. But I believe that this is only a momentary setback. The evidence and the moral grounds for eliminating poverty are too strong to ignore much longer.

The phrase "poverty amid prosperity" has been used over the decades to describe the economic paradox found in the United States. Let us recognize both the injustice and contradiction of this phrase. But let us also recognize the possibility of vanquishing this situation through the productive use of our prosperity to ultimately abolish American poverty. When the social historians look back to our time 100 years from now, my greatest hope is that they will be able to write that this was the beginning of the end of the poverty paradox.

CHAPTER 1

1. Mark Robert Rank, *Living on the Edge: The Realities of Welfare in America* (New York: Columbia University Press, 1994).
2. Mark Robert Rank, *One Nation, Underprivileged: Why American Poverty Affects Us All* (New York: Oxford University Press, 2004).
3. Mark Robert Rank, Thomas A. Hirschl, and Kirk A. Foster, *Chasing the American Dream: Understanding What Shapes Our Fortunes* (New York: Oxford University Press, 2014).
4. Mark Robert Rank, Lawrence M. Eppard, and Heather E. Bullock, *Poorly Understood: What America Gets Wrong About Poverty* (New York: Oxford University Press, 2021).

CHAPTER 2

1. Adam Smith, *An Inquiry Into the Nature and Causes of Wealth of Nations* (London: W. Strahan and T. Cadell, 1776).
2. World Bank, *Piecing Together the Poverty Puzzle* (Washington, DC: World Bank, 2018).
3. Amartya Sen, *Inequality Reexamined* (New York: Russell Sage Foundation, 1992).
4. Shatakshee Dhongde and Robert Haveman, "Spatial and Temporal Trends in Multidimensional Poverty in the United States Over the Last Decade," *Social Indicators Research* 163 (2022): 47–472; Sarah Halpern-Meekin, *Social Poverty: Low-Income Parents and the Struggle for Family and Community Ties* (New York: New York University Press, 2019).
5. United Nations Development Programme, *Human Development Report, 2020* (New York: United Nations, 2020).
6. For more background on President Johnson's War on Poverty and Great Society programs, see Irwin Unger, *The Best of Intentions: The Triumph and Failure of the Great Society Under Kennedy, Johnson and Nixon* (New York: Doubleday, 1996); Martha J. Bailey and Sheldon Danziger, *Legacies of the War on Poverty*

(New York: Russell Sage Foundation, 2013). For further information on President Johnson's Kerner Commission, see Steven M. Gillon, *Separate and Unequal: The Kerner Commission and the Unraveling of American Liberalism* (New York: Basic Books, 2018).

7. Lyndon B. Johnson, "President Lyndon B. Johnson's Annual Message to the Congress on the State of the Union, January 8, 1964," *Public Papers of the Presidents of the United States: Lyndon B. Johnson*, 1963–64, vol. 1, entry 91 (Washington, DC: U.S. Government Printing Office), pp. 112–118.

8. John Iceland, "Measuring Poverty: Theoretical and Empirical Considerations," *Measurement: Interdisciplinary Research and Perspectives* 3 (2005): 199–235; John Iceland, *Poverty in America: A Handbook* (Berkeley, CA: University of California Press, 2013).

9. Mark Robert Rank, *Confronting Poverty: Economic Hardship in the United States* (Thousand Oaks, CA: Sage, 2021).

10. Signe-Mary McKernan and Michael Sherraden, *Asset Building and Low-Income Families* (Washington, DC: Urban Institute Press, 2008).

11. Bruce D. Meyer and James X. Sullivan, "Annual Report on U.S. Consumption Poverty: 2018," American Enterprise Institute, October 18, 2019.

12. Zachary Parolin, Megan Curran Jordan Matsudaira, Jane Waldfogel, and Christopher Wimer, "Estimating Monthly Poverty Rates in the United States," No. 20415, Center on Poverty and Social Policy, Columbia University, 2021.

13. Timothy M. Smeeding, "Poverty Measurement," in *The Oxford Handbook of the Social Science of Poverty*, ed. David Brady and Linda M. Burton (New York: Oxford University Press, 2016), pp. 21–46.

14. For a descriptive history of her approach, see Gordon M. Fisher, "The Development and History of the Poverty Thresholds," *Social Security Bulletin* 55 (1992): 3–14; Molly Orschansky, "Counting the Poor: Another Look at the Poverty Profile," *Social Security Bulletin* 28 (1965): 3–29.

15. See Amy Glaismeir, "Living Wage Calculator," 2022, https://livingwage.mit.edu/ (accessed November 15, 2022).

16. U.S. Bureau of the Census, *Poverty in the United States: 2021* (Report Number P60-277) (Washington, DC: U.S. Government Printing Office, 2022).

17. U.S. Bureau of the Census, *Poverty in the United States*.

18. J. Tom Mueller, Matthew M. Brooks, and Jose D. Pacas, "Cost of Living Variation, Nonmetropolitan America, and Implications for the Supplemental Poverty Measure," *Population Research and Policy Review* 41 (2022): 1501–1523.

19. Fabian T. Pfeffer, Paula Fomby, and Noura Insolera, "The Longitudinal Revolution: Sociological Research at the 50-Year Milestone of the Panel Study of Income Dynamics," *Annual Review of Sociology* 46 (2020): 1–26.

20. U.S. Bureau of the Census, *Dynamics of Economic Well-Being: Poverty 2013–2016* (Report Number P70BR-172) (Washington, DC: U.S. Government Printing Office, 2021). U.S. Bureau of the Census, *Poverty Dynamics: 2017–2019* (Report Number B70BR-179) (Washington, DC: U.S. Government Printing Office, 2022).

21. Mary Jo Bane and David T. Ellwood, "Slipping Into and Out of Poverty: The Dynamics of Spells," *Journal of Human Resources* 21 (1986): 12.

22. Stephanie Riegg Cellini, Signe-Mary McKernan, and Caroline Ratcliffe, "The Dynamics of Poverty in the United States: A Review of Data, Methods, and Findings," *Journal of Policy Analysis and Management* 27 (2008): 577–605.

23. Mark R. Rank, "Alleviating Poverty," in *Toward a Livable Life: A 21st Century Agenda for Social Work*, ed. Mark Robert Rank (New York: Oxford University Press, 2020), pp. 45–69.

24. U.S. Bureau of the Census, *Dynamics of Economic Well-Being: Participation in Government Programs, 2009–2012: Who Gets Assistance?* (Report Number P70-141) (Washington, DC: U.S. Government Printing Office, 2015).

25. Mark R. Rank, "Exiting From Welfare: A Life Table Analysis," *Social Service Review* 59 (1985): 358–376.

26. Mark R. Rank, "The Dynamics of Welfare Use: How Long and How Often?," in *Poverty and Social Welfare in the United States*, ed. Donald Tomaskovic-Devey (Boulder, CO: Westview Press, 1988), pp. 177–193.

27. U.S. Bureau of the Census, 2020, Survey of Income and Program Participation (SIPP) Detailed Program Receipt Tables: 2020.

28. Bane and Ellwood, "Slipping Into and Out of Poverty," p. 11.

29. Ann Huff Stevens, "Transition Into and Out of Poverty in the United States," Policy Brief, Center for Poverty Research, vol. 1, no. 1, UC Davis.

30. Cellini et al., "Dynamics of Poverty."

31. Thomas Shapiro, *Toxic Inequality: How America's Wealth Gap Destroys Mobility, Deepens the Racial Divide, and Threatens Our Future* (New York: Basic Books, 2017).

32. Dennis H. Sullivan and Andrea L. Ziegert, "Family Poverty in Black and White: Results From a New Poverty Measure," *Review of Black Political Economy* 48 (2021): 410–454.

33. Paul A. Jargowsky, *Concentration of Poverty in the New Millennium: Changes in Prevalence, Composition, and Location of High Poverty Neighborhoods* (Report by the Century Foundation) (New Brunswick, NJ: New York and Rutgers Center for Urban Research and Education, 2015), p. 15.

34. Paul A. Jargowsky, "Racial and Economic Segregation in the US: Overlapping and Reinforcing Dimensions," in *Handbook of Urban Segregation*, ed. Sako Musterd (London: Edward Elgar, 2019), pp. 151–168.

35. Jargowsky, *Concentration of Poverty*, pp. 11–13.

36. Karin B. Anacker, *The New American Suburb: Poverty, Race and the Economic Crisis* (Burlington, VT: Ashgate, 2015); Karyn Lacy, "The New Sociology of Suburbs: A Research Agenda for Analysis of Emerging Trends," *Annual Review of Sociology* 42 (2016): 369–384; Elizabeth Mattiuzzi and Margaret Weir, *Overlooked Suburbs: The Changing Metropolitan Geography of Poverty in the Western United States* (Community Development Research Brief) (San Francisco: Federal Reserve Bank of San Francisco, 2022) pp. 160–161.

37. Elizabeth Kneebone and Alan Berube, *Confronting Suburban Poverty in America* (Washington, DC: Brookings Institution Press, 2013).

38. Kneebone and Berube, *Confronting Suburban Poverty*, p. 3.

39. Chris Hess, "Residential Segregation by Race and Ethnicity and the Changing Geography of Neighborhood Poverty," *Spatial Demography* 9 (2021): 57–106.

40. Lauren Gurley, "Who's Afraid of Rural Poverty? The Story Behind America's Invisible Poor," *American Journal of Economics and Sociology* 75 (2016): 589–604.

41. See Joseph Dalaker, "The 10-20-30 Provision: Defining Persistent Poverty Countries," *Congressional Research Service*, R45100, April 14, 2022; Joseph Dalaker, *The 10-20-30 Rule and Persistent Poverty Countries* (Congressional Research Service R44748) (Congressional Research Service, January 27, 2017).

42. Linda Labao, Minyu Zhou, Mark Parridge, and Michael Betz, "Poverty, Place, and Coal Employment: Across Appalachia and the United States in a New Economic Era," *Rural Sociology* 81 (2016): 343–386.

43. Angela Hattery and Earl Smith, "Social Stratification in the New/Old South: The Influences of Racial Segregation on Social Class in the Deep South," *Journal of Poverty* 11 (2007): 55–81; Heather O'Connell, Katherine J. Curtis, and Jack DeWaard, "Population Change and the Persistence of the Legacy of Slavery." Paper presented at the Rural Poverty Research Conference, Washington, DC, March 21–22, 2018.

44. Joan B. Anderson, "The U.S.–Mexican Border: A Half Century of Change," *Social Science Journal* 40 (2003): 535–554.

45. James J. Davis, Vincent J. Roscigno, and George Wilson, "American Indian Poverty in the Contemporary United States," *Sociological Forum* 31 (2015): 5–28; Whitney K. Mauer, "Indian Country Poverty: Place-Based Poverty on American Indian Territories, 2006–10," *Rural Sociology* 82 (2016): 473–498.

46. Philip Martin, Michael Fix, and J. Edward Taylor, *The New Rural Poverty: Agriculture and Immigration in California* (Washington, DC: Urban Institute Press, 2006).

47. James P. Ziliak, *Economic Change and the Social Safety Net: Are Rural Americans Still Behind"* (Discussion Paper Series, DP 2018-06) (Lexington, KY: University of Kentucky Center for Poverty Research, 2018).

48. Mark Robert Rank, Lawrence M. Eppard, and Heather E. Bullock, *Poorly Understood: What America Gets Wrong About Poverty* (New York: Oxford University Press, 2021), p. 23.

49. William Julius Wilson, "Urban Poverty, Race, and Space," in *The Oxford Handbook of the Social Science of Poverty*, ed. David Brady and Linda M. Burton (New York: Oxford University Press, 2016), pp. 394–413.

CHAPTER 3

1. Mark Robert Rank, Thomas A. Hirschl, and Kirk A. Foster, *Chasing the American Dream: Understanding What Shapes Our Fortunes* (New York: Oxford University Press, 2014); Robert C. Hauhart and Mitjz Sardoc, *The Routledge Handbook on the American Dream* (New York: Routledge, 2022); Jim Cullen, *The American Dream: A Short History of an Idea That Shaped a Nation* (New York: Oxford University Press, 2003).

2. Rank et al., *Chasing the American Dream*, p. 67.

3. Lawrence R. Samuel, *The American Dream: A Cultural History* (Syracuse, NY: Syracuse University Press, 2012); Sarah Churchwell, *Behold, America: The Entangled History of "America First" and the "American Dream"* (New York: Basic Books, 2018).

4. Lawrence M. Eppard, Mark Robert Rank, and Heather E. Bullock, *Rugged Individualism and the Misunderstanding of American Inequality* (Bethlehem, PA: Lehigh University Press, 2020); Herbert J. Gans, *Middle American Individualism: The Future of Liberal Democracy* (New York: Free Press, 1988).

5. David Hackett Fischer, *Albion's Seed: Four British Folkways in America* (New York: Oxford University Press, 1989).

6. Cullen, *The American Dream: A Short History*, p. 10.

7. Derek Bok, *The State of the Nation: Government and the Quest for a Better Society* (Cambridge, MA: Harvard University Press, 1996), p. 311.

8. Robert C. Hauhart and Mitja Sardox, "Introduction: What Is the American Dream?," in *The Routledge Handbook on the American Dream*, ed. Robert C. Hauhart and Mitja Sardoc (New York: Routledge, 2022), pp. 1–26; Norton Garfinkle, *The American Dream vs. The Gospel of Wealth: The Fight for a Productive Middle-Class Economy* (New Haven, CT: Yale University Press, 2006).

9. Crystal L. Hoyt, Jeni L. Burnette, Rachel B. Forsyth, Mitchell Parry, and Brenten H. DeShields, "Believing in the American Dream Sustains Negative Attitudes Toward Those in Poverty," *Social Psychology Quarterly* 84 (2021): 203–215.

10. Victor Tan Chen, "The Mirage of Meritocracy and the Morality of Grace," in *The Routledge Handbook on the American Dream*, ed. Robert C. Hauhart and Mitja Sardoc (New York: Routledge, 2022), pp. 58–72.

11. Matthew O. Hunt and Heather E. Bullock, "Ideologies and Beliefs About Poverty," in *The Oxford Handbook of the Social Science of Poverty*, ed. David Brady and Linda M. Burton (New York: Oxford University Press, 2016), pp. 93–116.

12. Eppard et al., *Rugged Individualism*.

13. Mark Robert Rank, *Living on the Edge: The Realities of Welfare in America* (New York: Columbia University Press, 1994); in addition, see Francesco Duina, *Broke and Patriotic: Why Poor Americans Love Their Country* (Stanford, CA: Stanford University Press, 2018).

14. Shai Davidai, "Why Do Americans Believe in Economic Mobility? Economic Inequality, External Attributions of Wealth and Poverty, and the Belief in Economic Mobility," *Journal of Experimental Psychology* 79 (2018): 138–148.

15. George Gilder, *Wealth and Poverty* (New York: Basic Books, 1981), p. 68.

16. Isabel V. Sawhill, "The Behavioral Aspects of Poverty," *Public Interest* 153 (2001): 83.

17. Davidai, "Why Do Americans Believe."

18. Richard J. Hernstein and Charles Murray, *The Bell Curve: Intelligence and Class Structure in American Life* (New York: Free Press, 1994).

19. Hernstein and Murray, *The Bell Curve*, pp. 193–194.

20. Michael B. Katz, *The Undeserving Poor: America's Enduring Confrontation With Poverty* (New York: Oxford University Press, 2013).

21. Charles Murray, *Coming Apart: The State of White America, 1960–2010* (New York: Crown Forum, 2012).

22. Mary O'Hare, *The Shame Game: Overturning the Toxic Poverty Narrative* (Bristol, UK: Policy Press, 2020); Lenette Azzi-Lessing, *Behind From the Start: How America's War on the Poor Is Harming Our Most Vulnerable Children* (New York: Oxford University Press, 2017).

23. Sasha Abramsky, *The American Way of Poverty: How the Other Half Still Lives* (New York: Nation Books, 2013).

24. Robert Walker, *The Shame of Poverty* (New York: Oxford University Press, 2014), p. 53.

25. Rank, *Living on the Edge*, p. 139.

26. Kathryn J. Edin and H. Luke Shaefer, *$2.00 a Day: Living on Almost Nothing in America* (New York: Hougton, Mifflin, Harcourt, 2015); Matthew Desmond, *Evicted: Poverty and Profit in the American City* (New York: Random House, 2016); Jason DeParle, *American Dream: Three Women, Ten Kids, and a Nation's Drive to End Welfare* (New York: Viking, 2004).

27. Mark R. Rank, "Why Poverty and Inequality Undermine Justice in America," in *Routledge International Handbook of Social Justice*, ed. Michael Reisch (New York: Routledge Press, 2014), pp. 436–447.

28. Charles Murray, *Losing Ground: American Social Policy 1950–1980* (New York: Basic Books, 1984); Lawrence M. Mead, *The New Politics of Poverty: The Nonworking Poor in America* (New York: Basic Books, 1992); Marvin Olasky, *The Tragedy of American Compassion* (Washington, DC: Regnery Publishing, 1992); Edward Conard, *The Upside of Inequality: How Good Intentions Undermine the Middle Class* (New York: Portfolio, 2016).

29. Karl Marx and Friedrich Engels, *Selected Works* (New York: International Publishers, 1968), pp. 86–87.

30. Marx and Engels, *Selected Works*, p. 94.

31. Eric O. Wright, *Interrogating Inequality: Essays on Class Analysis, Socialism, and Marxism* (London: Verso, 1994).

32. Mark R. Rank, "Alleviating Poverty," in *Toward a Livable Life: A 21st Century Agenda for Social Work*, ed. Mark Robert Rank (New York: Oxford University Press, 2020), pp. 45–69.

33. Harry J. Holzer, "Workforce Development Programs," in *Legacies of the War on Poverty*, ed. Martha J. Bailey and Sheldon Danziger (New York: Russell Sage Foundation, 2013), pp. 121–150; Tereas Sommer, Terri J. Sabol, Elise Chor, William Schneider, P. Lindsay Chase-Lansdale, Jeanne Brooks-Gunn, Mario L. Small, Christopher King, and Hirokazu Yoshikawa, "A Two-Generation Human Capital Approach to Antipoverty Policy," *Russell Sage Foundation Journal of the Social Sciences* 4 (2018): 118–143.

34. Besnik Pula, "Dual Labor Market/Dual Economy," in *The Wiley-Blackwell Encyclopedia of Social* Theory, ed. Bryan S. Turner, Chang Kyung-Sup, Cynthia F. Epstein, Peter Kivisto, J. Michael Ryan, and William Outhwaite (New York: John Wiley, 2017), https://onlinelibrary.wiley.com/doi/10.1002/9781118430873.est0098.

35. Randy Hodson and Robert J. Kaufman, "Economic Dualism: A Critical Review," *American Sociological Review* 47 (1982): 730.

36. Robert K. Merton, *Social Theory and Social Structure* (New York: Free Press, 1949), p. 50.

37. Herbert J. Gans, "Positive Functions of Poverty," *American Journal of Sociology* 78 (1972): 275–289; Herbert J. Gans, *People, Plans, and Policies: Essays on Poverty,*

Racism, and Other National Urban Problems (New York: Columbia University Press, 1991); Herbert J. Gans, "The Benefits of Poverty," *Challenge* 55 (2012): 114–125.

38. Gans, "Positive Functions of Poverty," p. 288.

39. Frances Fox Piven and Richard A. Cloward, *Regulating the Poor: The Functions of Public Welfare* (New York: Pantheon, 1971).

40. Carol B. Stack, *All Our Kin: Strategies for Survival in a Black Community* (New York: Harper and Row, 1974), pp. 127–128.

41. David Brady, *Rich Democracies, Poor People: How Politics Explain Poverty* (New York: Oxford University Press, 2009), pp. 5–6.

42. Brady, *Rich Democracies*, p. 6.

43. David Brady, Ryan M. Finnigan, and Sabine Hubgen, "Rethinking the Risks of Poverty: A Framework for Analyzing Prevalences and Penalties," *American Journal of Sociology* 123 (2017): 740–786.

44. David Brady, "Theories of the Causes of Poverty," *Annual Review of Sociology* 45 (2019): 155–175; David Brady, "Power Resource, Institutionalized Power Relations, and Poverty," in *On Inequality and Freedom*, ed. Lawrence M. Eppard and Henry A. Giroux (New York: Oxford University Press, 2022), pp. 156–168.

45. Oscar Lewis, *Five Families: Mexican Case Studies in the Culture of Poverty* (New York: Basic Books, 1959); Oscar Lewis, *La Vida: A Puerto Rican Family in the Culture of Poverty* (New York: Random House, 1966).

46. Oscar Lewis, "The Culture of Poverty," *Scientific American* 215 (1966): 19.

47. Lewis, "Culture of Poverty," p. 22.

48. Gordon B. Dahl, Andreas Raundal Kostol, and Magne Mogstad, "Family Welfare Culture," *Quarterly Journal of Economics* 129 (2017): 1711–1752.

49. Mario Luis Small, David J. Harding, and Michele Lamont, "Reconsidering Culture and Poverty," *Annals of the American Academy of Political and Social Science* 629 (2010): 6.

50. Samuel Bowles, Steven N. Durlauf, and Karla Huff, *Poverty Traps* (New York: Russell Sage Foundation, 2006).

51. William Julius Wilson, *The Truly Disadvantaged: The Inner City, the Underclass, and Public Policy* (Chicago: University of Chicago Press, 1987), p. 61.

52. Wilson, p. 57.

53. Wilson, p. 58.

54. Wilson, p. 137.

CHAPTER 4

1. Gary Becker, *Human Capital: A Theoretical and Empirical Analysis With Special Reference to Education* (Chicago: University of Chicago Press, 1993); Lynn Karoly, "Investing in the Future: Reducing Poverty Through Human Capital Investment," in *Understanding Poverty*, ed. Sheldon H. Danziger and Robert H. Haveman (New York: Russell Sage Foundation, 2001), pp. 314–356; Tereas Sommer, Terri J. Sabol, Elise Chor, William Schneider, P. Lindsay Chase-Lansdale, Jeanne Brooks-Gunn, Mario L. Small, Christopher King, and Hirokazu Yoshikawa, "A

Two-Generation Human Capital Approach to Antipoverty Policy," *Russell Sage Foundation Journal of the Social Sciences* 4 (2018): 118–143.

2. David B. Bills, Valentina Di Stasio, and Klarita Gerxhani, "The Demand Side of Hiring: Employers in the Labor Market," *Annual Review of Sociology* 43 (2017): 291–310.

3. Devah Pager, Bruce Western, and Bart Bonikowski, "Discrimination in a Low Wage Labor Market: A Field Experiment," *American Sociological Review* 74 (2009): 794.

4. Matthew Wiswall and Basit Zafar, "Preference for the Workplace, Investment in Human Capital, and Gender," *Quarterly Journal of Economics* 133 (2018): 457–507.

5. Francine D. Blau and Anne E. Winkler, *The Economics of Women, Men, and Work* (New York: Oxford University Press, 2017).

6. U.S. Census Bureau, *Poverty in the United States: 2021* (Report Number P60-277) (Washington, DC: U.S. Government Printing Office, 2022).

7. Eric A. Hanuschek and Ludger Woessmann, "Skills, Mobility, and Growth," in *Economic Mobility: Research and Ideas on Strengthening Families, Communities and the Economy*, ed. Federal Reserve Bank of St. Louis (Washington, DC: Board of Governors of the Federal Reserve System, 2017), pp. 421–449.

8. Mark R. Rank, "A Structural Vulnerability Understanding of American Poverty," in *On Inequality and Freedom*, ed. Lawrence M. Eppard and Henry A. Giroux (New York: Oxford University Press, 2022), pp. 126–145.

9. Federal Reserve System, "Report on the Economic Well-Being of U.S. Households in 2020–May 2021," 2021. https://www.federalreserve.gov/publications/files/2020-report-economic-well-being-us-households-202105.pdf.

10. Karen T. Seccombe, *So You Think I Drive a Cadillac?: Welfare Recipients' Perspectives on the System and Its Reform* (New York: Pearson, 2010).

11. Mark Robert Rank, *Living on the Edge: The Realities of Welfare in America* (New York: Columbia University Press, 1994), p. 57.

12. Lawrence M. Eppard, Mark Robert Rank, and Heather E. Bullock, *Rugged Individualism and the Misunderstanding of American Inequality* (Bethlehem, PA: Lehigh University Press, 2020); Amy Goldstein, *Janesville: An American Story* (New York: Simon and Schuster, 2017); Jonathan Morduch and Rachel Schneider, *The Financial Diaries: How American Families Cope in a World of Uncertainty* (Princeton, NJ: Princeton University Press, 2017).

13. Lillian B. Rubin, *Families on the Faultline: America's Working Class Speaks About the Family, the Economy, Race, and Ethnicity* (New York: HarperCollins, 1994), pp. 30–31.

14. Jacob S. Hacker, *The Great Risk Shift: The Assault on American Jobs, Families, Health Care, and Retirement and How You Can Fight Back* (New York: Oxford University Press, 2006).

15. Daniel A. Sandoval, Mark R. Rank, and Thomas A. Hirschl, "The Increasing Risk of Poverty Across the American Life Course," *Demography* 46 (2009): 717–737.

16. Mark Robert Rank, Thomas A. Hirschl, and Kirk A. Foster, *Chasing the American Dream: Understanding What Shapes Our Fortunes* (New York: Oxford University Press, 2014).

17. Arne L. Kalleberg, *Good Jobs, Bad Jobs: The Rise of Polarized and Precarious Employment Systems in the United States, 1970s to 2000s* (New York: Russell Sage Foundation, 2011).

18. Rank et al., *Chasing the American Dream*, 2014.

19. U.S. Census Bureau, *Poverty in the United States*.

20. Kalleberg, *Good Jobs, Bad Jobs*.

21. Hacker, *Great Risk Shift*; Charles Tilly, *Half a Job: Bad and Good Part-Time Jobs in a Changing Labor Market* (Philadelphia: Temple University Press, 2010); Lawrence F. Katz and Alan B. Krueger, "Understanding Trends in Alternative Work Arrangements in the United States," *Russell Sage Foundation Journal of the Social Sciences* 5 (2019): 132–146.

22. U.S. Bureau of Labor Statistics, "Employment Situation—January to December, 2021."

23. U.S. Bureau of Labor Statistics, "Employment Situation."

24. Kalleberg, *Good Jobs, Bad Jobs*.

25. Richard V. Reeves, *Dream Hoarders: How the American Upper Middle Class Is Leaving Everyone Else in the Dust, Why That Is a Problem, and What to Do About It* (Washington, DC: Brookings Institution Press, 2017).

26. Kalleberg, *Good Jobs, Bad Jobs*.

27. Raj Chetty, David Grusky, Maximillian Hell, Nathaniel Hendren, Robert Manduca, and Jimmy Narang, "The Fading American Dream: Trends in Absolute Income Mobility Since 1940," *Science* 356 (2017): 400.

28. Chetty et al., "Fading American Dream," p. 400.

29. Chetty et al., "Fading American Dream," p. 405.

30. Rank et al., *Chasing the American Dream*, pp. 71–72.

31. Rank et al., pp. 72–73.

32. James Midgley, *Inequality, Social Protection and Social Justice* (Cheltenham, UK: Edward Elgar, 2020); Gary Gerstel, *The Rise and Fall of the Neoliberal Order: America and the World in the Free Market Era* (New York: Oxford University Press, 2022); Monica Prasad, *Starving the Beast: Ronald Reagan and the Tax Cut Revolution* (New York: Russell Sage Foundation, 2018).

33. Kathryn J. Edin and H. Luke Shaefer, *$2.00 a Day: Living on Almost Nothing in America* (Boston: Houghton Mifflin Harcourt, 2015).

34. Rank et al., *Chasing the American Dream*, pp. 77–78.

35. Rank, *Living on the Edge*, p. 122.

36. Rank et al., *Chasing the American Dream*, pp. 120–121.

37. Walter Johnson, *The Broken Heart of America: St. Louis and the Violent History of the United States* (New York: Basic Books, 2020); Tony Messenger, *Profit and Punishment: How America Criminalizes the Poor in the Name of Justice* (New York: St. Martin's Press, 2021).

38. Joe R. Feagin, *Racist America: Roots, Current Realities, and Future Reparations* (New York: Routledge, 2010); Joe R. Feagin and Kimberley Ducey, "White Privilege and Black Burdens," in *On Inequality and Freedom*, ed. Lawrence M. Eppard and Henry A. Giroux (New York: Oxford University Press, 2022), pp. 205–240.

39. Marianne Bertand and Sendhil Mullainathan, "Are Emily and Greg More Employable Than Lakisha and Jamal? A Field Experiment on Labor Market Discrimination," *American Economic Review* 94 (2004): 991–1013.

CHAPTER 5

1. John Ermisch, Markus Jantti, and Timothy Smeeding, *From Parents to Children: The Intergenerational Transmission of Advantage* (New York: Russell Sage Foundation, 2012); Samuel Bowles, Herbert Gintis, and Melissa Osborne Groves, *Unequal Chances: Family Background and Economic Success* (New York: Russell Sage Foundation, 2005).
2. Bhaskar Mazumber, "Intergenerational Mobility in the United States: What We Have Learned from the PSID," *Annals of the American Academy of Political and Social Science* 680 (2018): 213–234.
3. Fabian T. Pfeffer and Alexandria Killewald, "Generations of Advantage: Multigenerational Correlations in Family Wealth," *Social Forces* 96 (2018): 1411–1442.
4. Lillian B. Rubin, *Families on the Faultline: America's Working Class Speaks About the Family, the Economy, Race, and Ethnicity* (New York: HarperCollins, 1994), p. 36.
5. See Mark Robert Rank, *Living on the Edge: The Realities of Welfare in America* (New York: Columbia University Press, 1994); Mark Robert Rank, *One Nation, Underprivileged: Why American Poverty Affects Us All* (New York: Oxford University Press, 2004); Mark Robert Rank, Thomas A. Hirschl, and Kirk A. Foster, *Chasing the American Dream: Understanding What Shapes Our Fortunes* (New York: Oxford University Press, 2014).
6. Robert K. Merton, "The Matthew Effect in Science: The Reward and Communication System of Science," *Science* 199 (1968): 55–63.
7. Robert K. Merton, "The Matthew Effect in Science, II: Cumulative Advantage and the Symbolism of Intellectual Property," *Isis* 79 (1988): 606.
8. Ermisch et al., *From Parents to Children*.
9. Paul A. Jargowsky, "Concentration of Poverty in the New Millennium: Changes in Prevalence, Composition, and Location of High Poverty Neighborhoods," A Report by the Century Foundation and Rutgers Center for Urban Research and Education, 2013, https://cure.camden.rutgers.edu/files/2013/12/Concentration_of_Poverty_in_the_New_Millennium.pdf.
10. Jeanne Brooks-Gunn, Greg J. Duncan, and Lawrence Aber, *Neighborhood Poverty: Context and Consequences for Children* (New York: Russell Sage Foundation, 1997); Gary W. Evans, "The Environment of Childhood Poverty," *American Psychologist* 56 (2004): 77–92; Mary Patillo and John N. Robinson, "Poor Neighborhoods in the Metropolis," in *The Oxford Handbook of the Social Sciences of Poverty*, ed. David Brady and Linda M. Burton (New York: Oxford University Press, 2016), pp. 341–368.
11. Margery Austin Turner and Deborah R. Kaye, *How Does Family Well-Being Vary Across Different Types of Neighborhoods?* Low-Income Working Families Series, Paper 6 (Washington, DC: Urban Institute, 2006), p. 20.

12. William Julius Wilson, *More Than Just Race: Being Black and Poor in the Inner City* (New York: W. W. Norton, 2009).

13. Douglas S. Massey, "Segregation and the Perpetuation of Disadvantage," in *The Oxford Handbook of the Social Sciences of Poverty*, ed. David Brady and Linda M. Burton (New York: Oxford University Press, 2016), pp. 369–393; Douglas S. Massey, "Still the Linchpin: Segregation and Stratification in the USA," *Race and Social Problems* 12 (2020): 1–12.

14. Robert J. Sampson, *Great American City: Chicago and the Enduring Neighborhood Effect* (Chicago: University of Chicago Press, 2012).

15. Sean F. Reardon and Kendra Bischoff, "Income Inequality and Income Segregation," *American Journal of Sociology* 116 (2011): 1092–1153.

16. Douglas S. Massey, "The Age of Extremes: Concentrated Affluence and Poverty in the Twenty-First Century," *Demography* 33 (1996): 395–412.

17. Lincoln Quillian, "How Long Are Exposures to Poor Neighborhoods? The Long-Term Dynamics of Entry and Exit From Poor Neighborhoods," *Population Research and Policy Review* 22 (2003): 221–249.

18. Patrick Sharkey, "The Intergenerational Transmission of Context," *American Journal of Sociology* 113 (2008): 931–969.

19. Mark R. Rank, "Measuring the Economic Racial Divide Across the Course of American Lives," *Race and Social Problems* 1 (2009): 57–66.

20. U.S. Census Bureau, *Wealth, Asset Ownership, and Debt of Households Detailed Tables: 2018*, September 17, 2021. https://www.census.gov/data/tables/2018/demo/wealth/wealth-asset-ownership.html.

21. Raj Chetty, Nathaniel Hendren, Maggie R. Jones, and Sonya R. Porter, "Race and Economic Opportunity in the United States: An Intergenerational Perspective," *Quarterly Journal of Economics* 135 (2020): 711–783.

22. Mark Robert Rank, *Confronting Poverty: Economic Hardship in the United States* (Newbury Park, CA: Sage, 2021).

23. Anne Case and Christina H. Paxson, "Children's Health and Social Mobility," *Future of Children* 16 (2006): 151–173.

24. Steven N. Durlauf, "Groups, Social Influences, and Inequality," in *Poverty Traps*, ed. Samuel Bowles, Steven N. Durlauf, and K. Hoff (New York: Russell Sage Foundation, 2006), p. 146.

25. Rank, *One Nation, Underprivileged*, p. 207.

26. Tama Leventhal and Jeanne Brooks-Gunn, "The Neighborhoods They Live In: The Effect of Neighborhood Residence on Child and Adolescent Outcomes," *Psychological Bulletin* 126 (2000): 309–337.

27. Richard D. Kahlenberg, *Economic School Integration: An Update* (Century Foundation Issue Brief Series) (New York: Century Foundation, 2002).

28. Steven N. Durlauf, "Groups, Social Influences, and Inequality," in *Poverty Traps*, ed. Samuel Bowles, Steven N. Durlauf, and K. Hoff (New York: Russell Sage Foundation, 2006), pp. 141–161; Steven N. Durlauf, "The Membership Theory of Poverty: The Role of Group Affiliations in Determining Socioeconomic Status," in *Understanding Poverty*, ed. Sheldon H. Danziger and Robert H. Haveman (New York: Russell Sage Foundation, 2001), pp. 392–416.

29. Jonathan Kozal, *Savage Inequalities: Children in America's Schools* (New York: Crown Publishers, 1991).

30. U.S. Department of Education, Equity and Excellence Commission, *For Each and Every Child: A Strategy for Education Equity and Excellence* (Washington, DC: Education Publications Center, 2013), p. 12.

31. Emily Hunnum and Yu Xie, "Education," in *The Oxford Handbook of the Social Sciences of Poverty*, ed. David Brady and Linda M. Burton (New York: Oxford University Press, 2016), pp. 462–485.

32. Jennifer Hochschild and Nathan Scovronick, *The American Dream and the Public Schools* (New York: Oxford University Press, 2003), pp. 12–13.

33. Erica Frankenberg, Jongyeon Ee, Jennifer B. Ayscue, and Gary Orfield, *Harming Our Common Future: America's Segregated Schools 65 Years After* Brown (Civil Rights Project, May 10, 2019) (University of California—Los Angeles), p. 9.

34. Frankenberg et al., *Harming Our Common Future*, p. 9.

35. Ann Owens, "Unequal Opportunity: School and Neighborhood Segregation in the USA," *Race and Social Problems* 12 (2020): 29–41.

36. Hochschild and Scovronick, *American Dream and the Public Schools*, p. 5.

37. Hochschild and Scovronick, *American Dream and the Public Schools*, p. 23.

38. Ermisch et al., *From Parents to Children*; Thomas M. Shapiro, *The Hidden Cost of Being African American: How Wealth Perpetuates Inequality* (New York: Oxford University Press, 2004).

39. Michelle Jackson and Brian Holzman, "A Century of Educational Inequality in the United States," *Proceedings of the National Academy of Sciences of the United States of America*, 117, no. 32 (2020): 19108–19115.

40. Daniel P. McMurrer and Isabel V. Sawhill, *Getting Ahead: Economic and Social Mobility in America* (Washington, DC: Urban Institute Press, 1998), p. 69.

41. Greg J. Duncan and Richard J. Murnane, *Whither Opportunity? Rising Inequality, Schools, and Children's Life Chances* (New York: Russell Sage Foundation, 2011), p. 15.

42. Arne L. Kalleberg, *Good Jobs, Bad Jobs: The Rise of Polarized and Precarious Employment Systems in the United States, 1970s to 2000s* (New York: Russell Sage Foundation, 2011), p. 80.

43. Sandra Susan Smith, "Job-Finding Among the Poor: Do Social Ties Matter?," in *The Oxford Handbook of the Social Sciences of Poverty*, ed. David Brady and Linda M. Burton (New York: Oxford University Press, 2016), pp. 438–461.

44. Kalleberg, *Good Jobs, Bad Jobs*, p. 181.

45. Joe R. Feagin, *Racist America: Roots, Current Realities, and Future Reparations* (New York: Routledge, 2010); in addition, see Nicholas Guyatt, *Bind Us Apart: How Enlightened Americans Invented Racial Segregation* (New York: Basic Books, 2016) for an examination of the early origins of racial segregation.

46. Rank, "Measuring the Economic Racial Divide."

47. Ronald J. Angel, "Social Class, Poverty and the Unequal Burden of Illness and Death," in *The Oxford Handbook of the Social Sciences of Poverty*, ed. David Brady and Linda M. Burton (New York: Oxford University Press, 2016), pp. 660–683.

48. Rank, *Confronting Poverty*.

49. Richard Wilkinson and Kate Pickett, *The Spirit Level: Why Greater Equality Makes Societies Stronger* (New York: Bloomsbury Press, 2010).

50. Richard Wilkinson and Kate Pickett, *The Inner Level: How More Equal Societies Reduce Stress, Restore Sanity and Improve Everyone's Well-Being* (New York: Penguin Press, 2019).

51. Jamie B. Royce, "The Effects of Poverty on Childhood Development," *Journal of Mental Health and Social Behavior* 3 (2021): 132.

52. David C. Wheeler, Joseph Boyle, Shyam Raman, and Erik J. Nelson, "Modeling Elevated Blood Lead Level Risk Across the United States," *Science of the Total Environment* 769 (2021): 145237.

53. Bradley R. Schiller, *The Economics of Poverty and Discrimination*, 10th ed. (Upper Saddle River, NJ: Prentice-Hall, 2008), p. 136.

54. Gopal K. Singh and Hyunjung Lee, "Marked Disparities in Life Expectancy by Education, Poverty Level, Occupation, and Housing Tenure in the United States, 1997–2014," *International Journal of Maternal and Child Health and AIDS* 10 (2021): 7.

55. Gregory Pappas, Susan Queen, Wilbur Hadden, and Gail Fisher, "The Increasing Disparity in Mortality Between Socioeconomic Groups in the United States, 1960 and 1986," *New England Journal of Medicine* 329 (1993): 103–115.

56. Raj Chetty, Michael Stepner, and Sarah Abraham, "The Association Between Income and Life Expectancy in the United States, 2001–2014," *JAMA* 315 (2016): 1750–1766.

57. Alina S. Schnake-Mahl, Pricila H. Mullacher, Jonathan Purtle, Ran Li, Ana V. Diez Roux, and Usama Bilal, "Heterogeneity in Disparities in Life Expectancy Across US Metropolitan Areas," *Epidemiology* 33 (2022): 890–899.

58. Corey M. Abramson, *The End Game: How Inequality Shapes Our Final Years* (Cambridge, MA: Harvard University Press, 2015).

59. Transamerica Center for Retirement Studies, "18th Annual Transamerica Retirement Survey: A Compendium of Findings About American Workers," June 2018.

60. Markus Jantti, Bernt Bratsberg, Knut Roed, Oddbjorn Raaum, Robin Naylor, Eva Osterbacka, Anders Bjorklund, and Tor Eriksson, *American Exceptionalism in a New Light: A Comparison of Intergenerational Earnings Mobility in the Nordic Countries, the United Kingdom and the United States* (Discussion Paper 1938) (Bonn, Germany: Institute for the Study of Labor, 2006).

61. Marie Connolly, Miles Corak, and Catherine Haeck, "Intergenerational Mobility Between and Within Canada and the United States," *Journal of Labor Economics* 52 (2019): 595–641.

62. Alan B. Krueger, "Economic Scene; The Apple Falls Close to the Tree, Even in the Land of Opportunity," *New York Times* November 14, 2002, Section C, p. 2.

63. Bhaskar Mazumder, "Intergenerational Mobility in the United States: What We Have Learned from the PSID," *Annals of the American Academy of Political and Social Science* 680 (2018): 213–234.

64. Michael Hout, "Americans Occupational Status Reflects Both of Their Parents," *Proceedings of the National Academy of Sciences of the United States of America* 115 (2018): 9527–9532.

65. McMurrer and Sawhill, *Getting Ahead*, p. 2.
66. Richard A. Bentron and Lisa A. Keister, "The Lasting Effect of Intergenerational Wealth Transfers: Human Capital, Family Formation, and Wealth," *Social Science Research* 68 (2017): 1–14; Alexandia Killewald, Fabian T. Pfeffer, and Jared N. Schachner, "Wealth Inequality and Accumulation," *Annual Review of Sociology* 43 (2017): 379–404; Fabian T. Pfeffer and Alexandra Killewald, "Intergenerational Wealth Mobility and Racial Inequality," *Socius* 5 (2019); Federal Reserve Bank of St. Louis, *Economic Mobility: Research and Ideas on Strengthening Families, Communities and the Economy* (Washington, DC: Board of Governors of the Federal Reserve System, 2017), pp. 385–420.
67. William G. Gale and John Karl Scholz, "Intergenerational Transfers and the Accumulation of Wealth," *Journal of Economic Perspectives* 8 (1994): 145–160.
68. Jagdeesh Gokhale and Lawrence J. Kotlikoff, "Simulating the Transmission of Wealth Inequality," *American Economic Review* 92 (2002): 268.
69. Greg J. Duncan and Richard J. Murnane, "Rising Inequality in Family Incomes and Children's Education Outcomes," *Russell Sage Foundation Journal of the Social Sciences* 2 (2016): 142–158; Kyle Crowder and Scott J. South, "Neighborhood Distress and School Dropout: The Variable Significance of Community Context," *Social Science Research* 32 (2003): 659–698.
70. Joan R. Rogers, "An Empirical Study of Intergenerational Transmission of Poverty in the United States," *Social Science Quarterly* 76 (1995): 178–194; see also Arthur Sakamoto, Li Hsu, and Mary E. Jalufka, "Comparing the Effects of Class Origins Versus Race in the Intergenerational Transmission of Poverty," *Social Sciences* 11 (2022): 257.
71. Thomas A. Hirschl and Mark R. Rank, "The Life Course Dynamics of Affluence," *PLoS One* 10 (2015): e0116370.
72. Miles Corak, *Chasing the Same Dream, Climbing Different Ladders: Economic Mobility in the United States and Canada* (Economic Mobility Project) (Philadelphia: Pew Charitable Trusts, 2010); Liana Fox, Florencia Torche, and Jane Waldfogel, "Intergenerational Mobility," in *The Oxford Handbook of the Social Science of Poverty*, ed. David Brady and Linda M. Burton (New York: Oxford University Press, 2016), pp. 528–554; Lawrence M. Eppard, Mark Robert Rank, and Heather E. Bullock, *Rugged Individualism and the Misunderstanding of American Inequality* (Bethlehem, PA: Lehigh University Press, 2020).
73. Raj Chetty, David Grusky, Maximilian Hell, Nathaniel Hendren, Robert Manduca, and Jimmy Narang, "The Fading American Dream: Trends in Absolute Mobility Since 1940," *Science* 356 (2017): 398–406; Jonathan David and Bhashkar Mazumder, *The Decline in Intergenerational Mobility After 1980*" (Working Paper No. WP-2017-5) (Chicago: Federal Reserve Bank of Chicago, 2020); Xi Song, Catherine G. Massey, Raken A. Rolf, Joseph P. Ferrie, Jonathan L. Rothman, and Yu Xie, "Long-Term Decline in Intergenerational Mobility in the United States Since the 1850s," *Proceedings of the National Academy of Sciences of the United States of America* 117 (2020): 251–258.
74. Florian Rolf Hertel and Fabian T. Pfeffer, "The Land of Opportunity? Trends in Social Mobility and Education in the United States," in *Social Mobility in Europe*

and the United States, ed. Richard Breen and Walter Muller (Stanford, CA: Stanford University Press, 2020), pp. 29–68.

75. Howard M. Wachtel, "Looking at Poverty From a Radical Perspective," *Review of Radical Political Economics* 3 (1971): 6.

CHAPTER 6

1. Michael B. Katz, *In the Shadow of the Poorhouse: A Social History of Welfare in America* (New York: Basic Books, 1996).
2. Mark R. Rank, "The Impact of the Covid-19 Pandemic Upon American Poverty" (Invited presentation given at the Global Health and Welfare Forum in Taiwan, Taipei, Taiwan, October 31–November 1, 2021).
3. Robert Haveman, Rebecca Blank, Robert Moffitt, Timothy Smeeding, and Geoffrey Wallace, "The War on Poverty: Measurement, Trends, and Policy," *Journal of Policy Analysis and Management* 34 (2015): 593–638.
4. Thomas J. Cottle, *Hardest Times: The Trauma of Long Term Unemployment* (Westport, CT: Praeger, 2001), p. 216.
5. Mark Robert Rank, Thomas A. Hirschl, and Kirk A. Foster, *Chasing the American Dream: Understanding What Shapes Our Fortunes* (New York: Oxford University Press, 2014), p. 69.
6. Martin Ross and Nicole Bateman, "Meet the Low-Wage Workforce," Metropolitan Policy Program at Brookings, Brookings Institution, November 2019. https://www.brookings.edu/wp-content/uploads/2019/11/201911_Brookings-Metro_low-wage-workforce_Ross-Bateman.pdf.
7. Arne L. Kalleberg, *Good Jobs, Bad Jobs: The Rise of Polarized and Precarious Employment Systems in the United States, 1970s to 2000s* (New York: Russell Sage Foundation, 2011); John N. Drobak, *Rethinking Market Regulation: Helping Labor by Overcoming Economic Myths* (New York: Oxford University Press, 2021); Jared Bernstein, *Crunch: Why Do I Feel So Squeezed? (and Other Unsolved Economic Mysteries)* (San Francisco: Berrett-Koehler Publishers, 2008).
8. Federal Reserve Economic Data, St. Louis Federal Reserve Board, 2022.
9. U.S. Bureau of Labor Statistics, "Employment Situation Summary. January–December 2021."
10. U.S. Bureau of Labor Statistics, "Work Experience of the Population (Annual) New Release" (December 14, 2018).
11. Abu Bakkar Siddique, "Poverty in the USA: The Role of Job Market Polarization and Job Quality," available at *SSRN* 38-8725 (2021).
12. Laurent Gobillon and Harris Selod, "Spatial Mismatch, Poverty, and Vulnerable Populations," in *Handbook of Regional Science*, ed. Manfred M. Fischer and Peter Nijkamp (New York: Springer, 2021), pp. 573–588; Christina Stacy and Brady Meixell, "The Changing Geography of Spatial Mismatch," *Cityscape* 22 (2020): 373–378; Martin Ruef and Angelina Grigoryeva, "Jim Crow and the Spatial Mismatch Hypothesis," *American Journal of Sociology* 126 (2020): 407–452.
13. William Julius Wilson, *When Work Disappears: The World of the New Urban Poor* (New York: Knopf, 1996), p. 37.

14. Katherine Newman, *No Shame in My Game: The Working Poor in the Inner City* (New York: Knopf, 1999); Katherine Newman, "The Subjective Meaning of Mobility and Its Implications for Policy Solutions," in *Economic Mobility: Research and Ideas on Strengthening Families, Communities and the Economy*, ed. Federal Reserve Bank of St. Louis (Washington, DC: Board of Governors of the Federal Reserve System, 2017), pp. 55–64.

15. Cynthia M. Duncan, *Worlds Apart: Poverty and Politics in Rural America* (New Haven, CT: Yale University Press, 2014).

16. Regina S. Baker, "The Historical Racial Regime and Racial Inequality in Poverty in the American South," *American Journal of Sociology* 127 (2022): 1721–1781.

17. Fabian T. Pfeffer, Paula Fomby, and Noura Insolera, "The Longitudinal Revolution: Sociological Research at the 50-Year Milestone of the Panel Study of Income Dynamics," *Annual Review of Sociology* 46 (2020): 1–26; Timothy M. Smeeding, "The PSID in Research and Policy," *Annals of the American Academy of Political and Social Science* 680 (2018): 29–47; David S. Johnson, Katherine A. McGonagle, Vicki A. Freedman, and Narayan Sastry, "Fifty Years of the Panel Study of Income Dynamics: Past, Present, and Future," *Annals of the American Academy of Political and Social Science* 680 (2018): 9–28.

18. Mark R. Rank and Thomas A. Hirschl, "The Likelihood of Experiencing Relative Poverty Across the Life Course," *PLoS One* 10 (2015): e01333513.

19. Rank et al., *Chasing the American Dream*.

20. Mark R. Rank and Thomas A. Hirschl, "The Economic Risk of Childhood in America: Estimating the Probability of Poverty Across the Formative Years," *Journal of Marriage and Family* 61 (1999): 1058–1067.

21. Mark R. Rank and Thomas A. Hirschl, "Estimating the Proportion of Americans Ever Experiencing Poverty During Their Elderly Years," *Journal of Gerontology: Social Sciences* 54B (1999): S184–S193.

22. C. Wright Mills, *The Sociological Imagination* (New York: Oxford University Press, 1959), p. 9.

23. Mark Robert Rank, Lawrence M. Eppard, and Heather E. Bullock, *Poorly Understood: What America Gets Wrong About Poverty* (New York: Oxford University Press, 2021).

24. Rank et al., *Poorly Understood*.

25. Charles Noble, *Welfare as We Knew It: A Political History of the American Welfare State* (New York: Oxford University Press, 1997), p. 3.

26. Jonathan Bradshaw, Yekaterina Chzhen, Gill Main, Bruno Martorano, Leonardo Menchini, and Chris de Neubourg, "Relative Income Poverty Among Children in Rich Countries," Innocenti Working Paper, IWP-2012-01, January 2012.

27. Max Roser and Esteban Ortiz-Ospina, "Income Inequality," Our World in Data, 2013, https://ourworldindata.org/income-inequality; in addition, wealth inequality has grown much wider in the United States compared to Europe, see Thomas Blanchet and Clara Martinez-Toledano, "Wealth Inequality Dynamics in Europe and the United States: Understanding the Determinants," April 1, 2022, New York University, https://www.stern.nyu.edu/sites/default/files/assets/docume nts/BM2022_Manuscript.pdf.

28. Laurie C. Maldonado and Rense Nieuwenhuis, "Single-Parent Family Poverty in 24 OECD Countries: A Focus on Market and Redistribution Strategies," Luxembourg Income Study Center Research Brief 2/2015, p. 10; file:///C:/Users/markr/Downloads/Maldonado%202015%20-%20%20-%20Single-Parent%20Family%20Poverty%20in%2024%20OECD%20Countries%20A%20Focus%20on%20Market%20and%20Redistribution%20Strategies%20(5).pdf.

29. David Brady, Ryan M. Finnigan, and Sabine Hubgen, "Rethinking the Risk of Poverty: A Framework for Analyzing Prevalences and Penalties," *American Journal of Sociology* 123 (2017): 740–786.

30. David Brady, "Theories of the Causes of Poverty," *Annual Review of Sociology* 45 (2019): 155–175.

31. Cheol-Sung Lee and In-Hoe Koo, "The Welfare States and Poverty," in *The Oxford Handbook of the Social Sciences of Poverty*, ed. David Brady and Linda M. Burton (New York: Oxford University Press, 2016), p. 715.

32. Kathryn J. Edin and H. Luke Shaefer, *$2.00 a Day: Living on Almost Nothing in America* (Boston: Houghton Mifflin Harcourt, 2015).

33. Peiyi Lu, Mack Shelley, and Yi-Long Liu, "Government Transfers and Poverty Alleviation Among Older Adults in the United States From 2002 to 2014," *Social Policy and Society* 20 (2021): 561–579.

34. Kathleen Romig, *Social Security Lifts More Americans Above Poverty Than Any Other Program* (Washington, DC: Center on Budget and Policy Priorities, 2018).

35. Romig, *Social Security Lifts.*

36. David Cooper and Elise Gould, "Financial Security of Elderly Americans at Risk," Economic Policy Institute, Briefing Paper #362, 2013, p. 3.

37. Joint Economic Committee Democrats, "Medicare: Protecting Seniors and Families," 2018, pp. 2–3, https://www.jec.senate.gov/public/_cache/files/5f4be5d9-b297-467a-948a-e7525d04f924/medicare-final.pdf.

38. Mark Robert Rank, *Living on the Edge: The Realities of Welfare in America* (New York: Columbia University Press, 1994), p. 127.

CHAPTER 7

1. Mark Robert Rank, *Toward a Livable Life: A 21st Century Agenda for Social Work* (New York: Oxford University Press, 2020).

2. Jessica L. Kimpell, "Republican Civic Virtue, Enlightened Self-Interest and Tocqueville," *European Journal of Political Theory* 14 (2015): 345–367.

3. Alexis de Tocqueville, *Democracy in America*, vol. 2 (New York: Knopf, 1994; originally published 1840).

4. Greg J. Duncan, Ariel Kalil, and Kathleen M. Zio-Guest, "Parental Income and Children's Life Course: Lessons From the Panel Study of Income Dynamics," *Annals of the American Academy of Political and Social Science* 680 (2018): 82–96.

5. Matthew Ridley, Gautam Rao, Frank Schlbach, and Vikram Patel, "Poverty, Depression, and Anxiety: Causal Evidence and Mechanisms," *Science* 370 (2020): eaay0214; Dhruv Khullar and Dav A. Chokshi, "Health, Income, and

Poverty: Where We Are and What Could Help," *Health Affairs* Health Policy Brief, October 4, 2018.

6. Lenette Azzi-Lesing, *Behind From the Start: How America's War on the Poor Is Harming Our Most Vulnerable Children* (New York: Oxford University Press, 2017); Ajay Chaudry and Christopher Wimer, "Poverty Is Not Just an Indicator: The Relationship Between Income, Poverty, and Child Well-Being," *Academic Pediatrics* 16 (2016): S23–S29.

7. David Wood, "Effect of Child and Family Poverty on Child Health in the United States," *Pediatrics* 112 (2003): 707–711; Benjamin A. Gitterman, Patricia J. Flanagan, William H. Cotton, Kimberley J. Diley, James H. Duffee, Andrea E. Green, Virginia A. Keane, Scott D. Krugman, Julie M. Linton, Carla D. McKelvey, and Jacqueline L. Nelson, "Poverty and Child Health in the United States," *Pediatrics* 137 (2016); John Pascoe et al., "Mediators and Adverse Effects of Child Poverty in the United States," *Pediatrics* 137 (2016); Greg J. Duncan, Katherine Mgnuson, and Elizabeth Votruba-Drzal, "Moving Beyond Correlations in Assessing the Consequences of Poverty," *Annual Review of Psychology* 68 (2017): 413–434.

8. Harry J. Holzer, Diane Whitmore Schanzenback, Greg J. Duncan, and Jens Ludwig, "The Economic Costs of Childhood Poverty in the United States," *Journal of Children and Poverty* 14 (2008): 41–61; Children's Defense Fund, "Ending Child Poverty Now," 2019, https://www.childrensdefense.org/wp-content/uploads/2019/04/Ending-Child-Poverty-2019.pdf.

9. Arloc Sherman, *Wasting America's Future: The Children's Defense Fund Report on the Costs of Child Poverty* (Boston: Beacon Press, 1994), p. 99.

10. Michael McLaughlin and Mark R. Rank, "Estimating the Economic Cost of Childhood Poverty in the United States," *Social Work Research* 42 (2018): 73–83.

11. Martin Ravallion, *The Economics of Poverty* (New York: Oxford University Press, 2016).

12. Mark Robert Rank, Thomas A. Hirschl, and Kirk A. Foster, *Chasing the American Dream: Understanding What Shapes Our Fortunes* (New York: Oxford University Press, 2014).

13. Edward D. Kleinbard, *What's Luck Got To Do With It? How Smarter Government Can Rescue the American* Dream (New York: Oxford University Press, 2021), p. 173.

14. Rank et al., *Chasing the American Dream*, p. 109.

15. Vanessa D. Fabbre, Eleni Gaveras, Anna Goldfarb Shabsin, Janelle Gibson, and Mark Robert Rank, "Confronting Stigma, Discrimination, and Social Exclusion," in *Toward a Livable Life: A 21st Century Agenda for Social Work*, ed. Mark Robert Rank (New York: Oxford University Press, 2020), pp. 70–93.

16. Mark R. Rank, "Why Poverty and Inequality Undermine Justice in America," in *The Routledge International Handbook of Social Justice*, ed. Michael Reisch (New York: Routledge, 2014), pp. 436–447.

17. Cathleen Burnett, "Justice: Myth and Symbol," *Legal Studies Forum* 11 (1987): 79.

18. Walter I. Trattner, *From Poor Law to Welfare State: A History of Social Welfare in America* (New York: Free Press, 1999); Michael B. Katz, *In the Shadow of the Poorhouse: A Social History of Welfare in America* (New York: Basic Books, 1986).

19. Mark Robert Rank, Lawrence M. Eppard, and Heather B. Bullock, *Poorly Understood: What America Gets Wrong About Poverty* (New York: Oxford University Press, 2021).

20. Lyndon B. Johnson, "The President's Inaugural Address, January 20, 1965," vol. 1, entry 27, pp (Washington, DC: U.S. Government Printing Office), pp. 71–74.

21. Sanford Lakoff, *Democracy: History, Theory, Practice* (Boulder, CO: Westview Press, 1996).

22. Thomas W. Simon, *Democracy and Social Justice* (Lanham, MD: Rowman and Littlefield, 1995), p. 145.

23. Stephen M. Caliendo, *Inequality in America: Race, Poverty, and Fulfilling Democracy's Promise* (New York: Routledge, 2021).

24. Leonard Beeghley, *The Structure of Social Stratification in the United States* (Boston: Allyn and Bacon, 2000), p. 137.

25. Stephen Pimpare, *Politics for Social Workers: A Practical Guide to Effecting Change* (New York: Columbia University Press, 2022).

26. John S. Dryzek, *Democracy in Capitalist Times: Ideals, Limits, and Struggles* (New York: Oxford University Press, 1996).

27. Hannah Arendt, *On Revolution* (New York: Viking), pp. 63–64.

28. Amartya Sen, *Development as Freedom* (New York: Random House, 1999); Sarah K. Bruch, Myra Marx Ferree, and Joe Soss, "From Policy to Polity: Democracy, Paternalism, and the Incorporation of Disadvantaged Citizens," *American Sociological Review* 75 (2010); 205–226.

29. Simon, *Democracy and Social Justice*, pp. 170–171.

CHAPTER 8

1. Ron Haskins and Matt Weidinger, "The Temporary Assistance for Needy Families Program: Time for Improvements," *Annals of the American Academy of Political and Social Science* 686 (2019): 286–309.

2. Sehun Oh, Diana M. Dinitto, and Yeonwoo Kim, "Exiting Poverty: A Systematic Review of U.S. Postsecondary Education and Job Skills Training Programs in the Post-Welfare Reform Era," *International Journal of Sociology and Social Policy* 41 (2021): 1210–1226.

3. Marco Rubio, "Reclaiming the Land of Opportunity: Conservative Reforms for Combating Poverty," 2014, https://www.rubio.senate.gov/public/index.cfm/2014/1/rubio-delivers-address-on-50th-anniversary-of-the-war-on-poverty.

4. Lane Kenworthy, *Social Democratic Capitalism* (New York: Oxford University Press, 2020).

5. National Center for Education Statistics, "Back to School Statistics," 2022, https://nces.ed.gov/fastfacts/display.asp?id=372.

6. Jennifer Hochschild and Nathan Scovronick, *The American Dream and the Public Schools* (New York: Oxford University Press, 2003); Heather Beth Johnson, *The American Dream and the Power of Wealth: Choosing Schools and Inheriting Inequality in the Land of Opportunity* (New York: Routledge, 2006).

7. Linda Darling-Hammond and Laura Post, "Inequality in Teaching and Schooling Supporting High-Quality Teaching and Leadership in Low-Income Schools," in *A Nation at Risk: Preserving Public Education as an Engine for Social Mobility*, ed. Richard D. Kalenberg (New York: Century Foundation Press, 2000), p. 127.

8. Greg J. Duncan and Richard J. Murnane, *Whither Opportunity? Rising Inequality, Schools, and Children's Life Chances* (New York: Russell Sage Foundation, 2011).

9. Craig Jerald, *New York Times*, Education Trust, August 9, 2002.

10. Ronald J. Angel, "Social Class, Poverty and the Unequal Burden of Illness and Death," in *The Oxford Handbook of the Social Science of Poverty*, ed. David Brady and Linda M. Burton (New York: Oxford University Press, 2016), p. 671.

11. Jennifer Prah Ruger, *Health and Social Justice* (New York: Oxford University Press, 2010); Karen Seccombe and Kim A. Hoffman, *Just Don't Get Sick: Access to Health Care in the Aftermath of Welfare Reform* (New Brunswick, NJ: Rutgers University Press, 2007).

12. U.S. Bureau of the Census, *Health Insurance Coverage in the United States: 2021* (Report Number P60-278) (Washington, DC: Government Printing Office, 2022).

13. Heeju Sohn, "Racial and Ethnic Disparities in Health Insurance Coverage: Dynamics of Gaming and Losing Coverage Over the Life-Course," *Population Research and Policy Review* 36 (2017): 181–201.

14. U.S. Bureau of the Census, *Health Insurance Coverage*.

15. Jennifer Tolbert, Kendal Orgera, and Anthony Damico, *Key Facts About the Uninsured Population* (Issue Brief) (Kaiser Family Foundation, November 6, 2020), https://www.kff.org/uninsured/issue-brief/key-facts-about-the-uninsured-pop ulation/ .

16. Office of the Legislative Counsel, *Compilation of Patient Protection and Affordable Care Act* (Washington, DC: U.S. Government Printing Office, 2010).

17. Gerald F. Anderson, Peter Hussey, and Varduhi Petrosyan, "It's Still the Prices, Stupid: Why the US Spends So Much on Health Care, and a Tribute to Uwe Reinhardt," *Health Affairs* 38 (2019): 87–95.

18. Matthew Desmond, "Heavy Is the House: Rent Burden Among the American Urban Poor," *International Journal of Urban and Regional Research* 42 (2018): 160–170.

19. Joint Center for Housing Studies of Harvard University, *America's Rental Housing 2017* (Cambridge, MA: Harvard University, 2017).

20. National Low Income Housing Coalition, "Out of Reach 2022," file:///C:/Users/ markr/Downloads/2022_OOR.pdf.

21. National Low Income Housing Coalition, "Out of Reach."

22. Amy Glasmeir, "MIT Living Wage Calculator," 2022, https://livingwage.mit.edu/.

23. Millennial Housing Commission, *Meeting Our Nation's Housing Challenges* (Washington, DC: Bipartisan Millennial Housing Commission, 2002), p. iv.

24. Peter A. Kemp, "Housing Programs," in *The Oxford Handbook of the Social Science of Poverty*, ed. David Brady and Linda M. Burton (New York: Oxford University Press, 2016), pp. 820–842.

25. Alicia Mazzara and Brian Knudsen, "Where Families With Children Use Housing Vouchers: A Comparative Look at the 50 Largest Metropolitan Areas," Center on

Budget and Policy Priorities, January 3, 2019, https://www.cbpp.org/sites/default/files/atoms/files/1-3-19hous.pdf.

26. Michael Sherraden, *Assets and the Poor: A New American Welfare Policy* (New York: M. E. Sharpe, 1991).

27. Michael Sherraden, *Financial Capability and Asset Building for All*, Grand Challenges for Social Work Initiative, Working Paper No. 13, pp. 1–30, 2015, American Academy of Social Work and Social Welfare, Washington, DC.

28. Stephen Roll, Michal Grinstein-Weiss, Joseph Steensma, and Ann DeRuyter, "Developing Financial Assets for Lower-Income Households," in *Toward a Livable Life: A 21st Century Agenda for Social Work*, ed. Mark Robert Rank (New York: Oxford University Press, 2020), pp. 114–151.

29. Thomas M. Shapiro and Edward N. Wolff, *Assets for the Poor: The Benefits of Spreading Asset Ownership* (New York: Russell Sage Foundation, 2001).

30. Trina Williams, *The Homestead Act: A Major Asset-Building Policy in American History*, Working Paper 00-9 (St. Louis, MO: Center for Social Development, Washington University, 2000).

31. Suzanne Mettler, *Soldier to Citizens: The G.I. Bill and the Making of the Greatest Generation* (New York: Oxford University Press, 2005).

32. Suzanne Mettler, "Bringing the State Back Into Civic Engagement," *American Political Science Review* 96 (2002): 351–365.

33. U.S. Census Bureau, *The Wealth of Households: 2017* (Report Number P70BR-170) (Washington DC: U.S. Government Printing Office, 2020).

34. Center on Budget and Policy Priorities, "Policy Basics: Federal Tax Expenditures," December 8, 2020, https://www.cbpp.org/research/federal-tax/federal-tax-expenditures.

35. Roll et al., "Developing Financial Assets."

36. National Center for Employee Ownership, "Employee Ownership by the Numbers," September 2019.

37. William A. Darity and A. Kirsten Mullen, *From Here to Equality: Reparations for Black Americans in the Twenty-First Century* (Chapel Hill, NC: University of North Carolina Press, 2020).

38. Ellora Derenoncourt, Chi Hyun Kim, Moritz Kuhn, and Moritz Schularick, *Wealth of Two Nations: The U.S. Racial Wealth Gap, 1860–2020*, NBER Working Paper No. 30101 (Cambridge, MA: National Bureau of Economic Research, 2022), https://www.nber.org/papers/w30101; see also U.S. Census Bureau, "Wealth, Asset Ownership, and Debt of Households Detailed Tables: 2019,". https://www.census.gov/data/tables/2019/demo/wealth/wealth-asset-ownership.html

39. Derenoncourt et al., *Wealth of Two Nations*," pp. 3–4.

40. Regina S. Baker and Heather A. O'Connell, "Structural Racism, Family Structure, and Black-White Inequality: The Differential Impact of the Legacy of Slavery on Poverty Among Single Mother and Married Parent Households," *Journal of Marriage and Family* 84 (2022): 1341–1365.

41. Bradley R. Schiller, *The Economics of Poverty and Discrimination*, 10th ed. (Upper Saddle River, NJ: Prentice Hall, 2008), p. 296.

42. Tolbert et al., *Key Facts*.

43. Timothy M. Smeeding, Lee Rainwater, and Gary Burtless, "U.S. Poverty in a Cross-National Context," in *Understanding Poverty*, ed. Sheldon H. Danziger and Robert H. Haveman (Cambridge, MA: Harvard University Press, 2001), pp. 27–68.

44. Richard V. Burkhauser and Kevin Corinth, *The Minimum Wage Versus the Earned Income Tax Credit for Reducing Poverty* (IZA World of Labor, 2021), Insititute of Labor Economics, Bonn, Germany.

45. Center on Budget and Policy Priorities, *Child Tax Credit and Earned Income Tax Credit Lift 10.6 Million People Out of Poverty in 2018*, Off the Charts: Policy Insight Beyond the Numbers, October 31, 2019, Washington, DC.

46. Ann Pettifor, *The Case for the Green New Deal* (London: Verso, 2020).

47. David T. Ellwood and Elisabeth D. Welty, "Public Service Employment and Mandatory Work: A Policy Whose Time Has Come and Gone and Come Again?," in *Finding Jobs: Work and Welfare Reform*, ed. David E. Card and Rebecca M. Blank (New York: Russell Sage Foundation, 2000), pp. 299–372.

48. Hyman P. Minsky, *Stabilizing an Unstable Economy* (New Haven, CT: Yale University Press, 1986).

49. Lane Kenworthy, *Social Democratic America* (New York: Oxford University Press, 2014); Lane Kenworthy, *Would Democratic Socialism Be Better?* (New York: Oxford University Press, 2022).

50. Rebecca M. Blank, *It Takes a Nation: A New Agenda for Fighting Poverty* (Princeton, NJ: Princeton University Press, 1997), pp. 141–142.

51. Kenworthy, *Would Democratic Socialism*, p. 121.

52. State of Alaska: Department of Revenue, "Permanent Fund Dividend," 2021, https://pfd.alaska.gov/.

53. Louise Haagh, *The Case for Universal Basic Income* (New York: John Wiley and Sons, 2019).

54. Jeff Madrick, *Invisible Americans: The Tragic Cost of Child Poverty* (New York: Alfred A. Knop, 2020), pp. 134–135.

55. Zacahary Parolin, Sophie Collyer, and Megan A. Curran, Absence of Monthly Child Tax Credit Leads to 3.7 Million More Children in Poverty in January 2022, Columbia University Center Poverty and Social Policy Brief (New York City: Columbia University, February 17, 2022); see also Laura Wheaton, Linda Giannarelli, and Ilham Dehy, *2021 Poverty Projections: Assessing the Impact of Benefits and Stimulus Measures*, Urban Institute Research Report (Washington, DC: Urban Institute, July 2021).

56. Jason Deparle, "Monthly Payments to Families With Children to Begin," *New York Times*, August 2, 2021.

57. Kristina C. Miler, *Poor Representation: Congress and the Politics of Poverty in the United States* (New York: Cambridge University Press, 2018).

58. Jake Rosenfeld, "US Labor Studies in the Twenty-First Century: Understanding Laborism Without Labor," *Annual Review of Sociology* 45 (2019): 449–465.

59. Rosenfeld, "US Labor Studies."

60. Jake Rosenfeld and Jennifer Laird, "Unions and Poverty," in *The Oxford Handbook of the Social Science of Poverty*, ed. David Brady and Linda M. Burton (New York: Oxford University Press, 2016), p. 816.

61. Richard Freeman, Eunice Han, David Madland, and Brendan V. Duke, "How Does Declining Unionism Affect the American Middle Class and Intergenerational Mobility," in *Economic Mobility: Research and Ideas on Strengthening Families, Communities and the Economy*, ed. Federal Reserve Bank of St. Louis (Washington, DC: Board of Governors of the Federal Reserve System, 2017), pp. 451–480.

62. Rosenfeld, "US Labor Studies."

63. Edwin Amenta and Francesca Poletta, "The Cultural Impacts of Social Movements," *Annual Review of Sociology* 45 (2019): 279–299.

64. Frances Fox Piven and Lorraine C. Minnite, "Poor People's Politics," in *The Oxford Handbook of the Social Science of Poverty*, ed. David Brady and Linda M. Burton (New York: Oxford University Press, 2016), p. 765.

65. Hahrie Han, Elizabeth McKenna, and Michelle Oyakawa, *Prisms of the People: Power and Organizing in Twenty-First-Century America* (Chicago: University of Chicago Press, 2021).

66. Paul Roget Loeb, *Soul of a Citizen: Living With Conviction in a Cynical Time* (New York: St. Martin's Griffin, 1999), p. 219.

CHAPTER 9

1. Alice O'Connor, *Poverty Knowledge: Social Science, Social Policy, and the Poor in Twentieth-Century U.S. History* (Princeton, NJ: Princeton University Press, 2001), p. 9.

2. Kai Erikson, "On Sociological Prose," in *The Rhetoric of Social Research: Understood and Believed*, ed. Albert Hunter (New Brunswick, NJ: Rutgers University Press, 1990) p. 28.

3. Mark Robert Rank, Lawrence M. Eppard, and Heather E. Bullock, *Poorly Understood: What America Gets Wrong About Poverty* (New York: Oxford University Press, 2021).

4. Michael Levitin, *Generation Occupy: Reawakening American Democracy* (New York: Counterpoint, 2021).

5. Laura Wheaton, Linda Giannarelli, and Ilham Dehry, *2021 Poverty Projections: Assessing the Impact of Benefits and Stimulus Measures* (Urban Institute Research Report) (Washington, DC: Urban Institute, July 2021).

6. A similar sentiment was expressed by the former governor of Illinois, John Peter Altgeld, in March 1902. He had concluded a speech with the words: "Wrong may seem to triumph. Right may seem to be defeated. But the gravitation of eternal justice is upward toward the throne of God. Any political institution if it is to endure must be plum with that line of justice." As he left the stage, he collapsed from a cerebral hemorrhage and died. See Jeff Nussbaum, *Undelivered: The Never-Heard Speeches That Would Have Rewritten History* (New York: Flatiron Books, 2022), p. 203.

7. Yascha Mounk, *The Great Experiment: Why Diverse Democracies Fall Apart and How They Can Endure* (New York: Penguin Press, 2022); for a global perspective on progress toward greater equality, see Thomas Piketty, *A Brief History of Equality* (Cambridge, MA: Harvard University Press, 2022).

8. Eric Foner, *The Story of American Freedom* (New York: Norton, 1998), p. 225.

9. An interesting side note is that the phrases "freedom from want" and "freedom from fear" had actually appeared in the records of the Massachusetts Bay Colony in the 17th century. See David Hackett Fischer, *Albion's Seed: Four British Folkways in America* (New York: Oxford University Press, 1989), p. 879.

10. Cass R. Sunstein, *The Second Bill of Rights: FDR's Unfinished Revolution and Why We Need It More Than Ever* (New York: Basic Books, 2004), pp. 242–243.

For the benefit of digital users, indexed terms that span two pages (e.g., 52–53) may, on occasion, appear on only one of those pages.

Tables and figures are indicated by *t* and *f* following the page number